Scots Worship

Scots Worship

Lent, Holy Week and Easter

David D. Ogston

Edited by
Johnston McKay

SAINT ANDREW PRESS
Edinburgh

First published in 2013 by
SAINT ANDREW PRESS
121 George Street
Edinburgh EH2 4YN

Copyright © David Ogston

ISBN 978-0-86153-787-7

British Library Cataloguing in Publication Data

A catalogue record for this book is available from the
British Library.

It is the publisher's policy to only use papers that are
natural and recyclable and that have been manufactured
from timber grown in renewable, properly managed
forests. All of the manufacturing processes of the papers
are expected to conform to the environmental regulations
of the country of origin.

Typeset by Regent Typesetting, London
Printed and bound in the United Kingdom by
CPI Group (UK) Ltd

Contents

Acknowledgements

Thanks are due to:

Wild Goose Publications for permission to quote from George MacLeod, *The Whole Earth Shall Cry Glory*.

The Guildry Incorporation of Perth, and the Drummond, Forteviot, and Jimmie Cairncross Charitable Trusts for generous financial support.

Ann Crawford of Saint Andrew Press for help, advice and encouragement in the preparation.

Moira McGregor for providing a typescript of much of what David Ogston wrote in longhand until he reluctantly abandoned the fountain pen for a word-processor.

Preface

Words, spoken and written, were essential to David. Only David thought that packing for his summer holiday was complete if he had pen, paper, two poetry books and his copy of *Henry V*. This was to enable him to learn another chapter by heart, because he loved the language. David was only without a pen in his hand when he was cooking or digging his garden. In retirement, when he acquired a share of an allotment, he saw another writing opportunity, starting a monthly allotment newsletter written as if he was a monk toiling in the monastery garden! In playing with words in the writing of poems, prayers, liturgies and broadcast scripts, he demonstrated his love of language. This was first nurtured in the village school of Clochan by the dominie Hugh Milne. Even when critically ill in hospital, David asked for pen and paper.

After David's so sudden death in September 2008, many friends expressed the hope that his writings would not be lost. I gratefully acknowledge this encouragement – but translating that hope into reality is due to the love and support given to me by David's friend Johnston McKay. Johnston immediately offered to guide this project from start to finish. He read and edited all the papers David left and did everything to ensure the publication of this book. So it is to Johnston that I owe a debt of gratitude that is impossible to repay.

David had many favourite books. One was *Frederick* – not a historical tale of a long-ago figure, but a children's picture book of a wee mouse. Frederick fails to gather nuts for the winter hibernation; instead, he stores up memories of summer. During the long winter months, he uses words to paint pictures of these summer days, thereby encouraging the other mice to believe that the sun will shine again. How apt that David loved that wee story book. An Icelandic saying tells us: 'When everything is stripped away, all that is left is love and storytelling.'

Meg Ogston

Introduction

David Ogston was one of the most creative leaders of worship in the Church of Scotland. He was born and brought up in Aberdeenshire, and he never lost his love of the Doric language of his youth. Several parts of this collection reflect that. They also reflect two other of his passions: the liturgy of the Orthodox Church, and the use of the poetic at the centre of Holy Communion in worship.

After an assistantship in St Giles' Cathedral, David was minister of Balerno on the outskirts of Edinburgh for seven years until he was called in 1980 to the historic Kirk of St John the Baptist in the city of Perth. He was there for 27 years until ill-health led to retirement and his all-too-early death. David always acknowledged that St John's gave him the space and the atmosphere in which he could give expression to that deep love of liturgy. He began holding a Communion service at 9:30 on Sunday mornings, and for him this was not something for which he was responsible: it was an act of worship that sustained him personally and in his ministry.

When I was in charge of religious broadcasting on radio for BBC Scotland, I turned to David frequently to write and present a number of series of programmes of experimental worship for radio. He was the most brilliant contributor: he very quickly recognized that the fusion of his words and specifically chosen music on a theme gave far more opportunities to speak to the listener in the tone which is natural on radio, unlike the oratory of the set-piece sermon in a church service. He became more and more convinced that some of the radio style should be used in his Sunday worship. In particular, what he said at the Sunday morning Communion was expressed in that conversational style: absolutely right for the smaller gathering.

After David's death, his widow Meg and I were approached by countless people asking, in fact pleading, that some of his work should be published. This has taken some time to happen, partly because the sheer amount of material which David left was staggering. It was in almost every literary genre possible – and to make a selection for this book has been very difficult, to say the least. Making choices where excellence is standard has not been easy. However, it has had one huge compensation. I have found my own thinking and theology stimulated, though the drawback was that I often stopped editing the material and sat for a long time reflecting on it!

This book begins not with a formal contribution on the themes of Lent, Holy Week and Easter but with David's own description in three broadcasts of the breakdown he experienced. I defy anyone, however, to say that it is not the most powerful expression of a man's experience of what these great themes say Jesus shared with us. Harry Williams, another creative writer and preacher, who also experienced breakdown, once wrote about the true wilderness being what each of us experiences when we are alone with ourselves. He called his autobiography *Some Day I'll Find You*. David concludes that, without the breakdown, he would 'not have met himself'.

At the time of his death, David had begun selecting material for a book. It has been a privilege to help Meg to realize his wish.

Johnston McKay

A Strange Place (1)

On Passion Sunday 2001, I entered a strange place. Standing at the Communion table, just after the point in the service when the bread has been broken, I was aware that my sense of balance had gone. The solid floor beneath my feet was no longer solid; I found myself clinging to the table like someone in a bed of quicksand holding on to a rock. I felt that if I left the table to serve the bread to the people in the pews, as I was meant to do, I would probably fall down. I shuffled sideways and muttered to our student, Joanne, that I wasn't feeling too well – and I left the chapel. In the vestry, our beadle, Jack, made me strong, sweet tea. But the tea didn't help. The strange place was beginning to happen, and it would be eight months before I would stand again at the table and say the words: 'This is my body, broken for you.'

That cold March day (my birthday, as it happened), my body was speaking to me. I had no choice but to listen. For weeks after that day, I would sit in the car at traffic lights listening to my fear, my nerves jangling. In queues in supermarkets, when an old lady discovered that she had picked up a tin of crushed pineapple when it was pineapple rings she really wanted, and an assistant had to go and fetch the required item, the banshees wailed inside me, though outwardly I looked calm and in control. I could no more face a visit to the town centre than I could contemplate walking on red-hot coals, so I would drive my wife to a car-park and wait for her to do the shopping, longing all the while to be home again.

My body was talking to me. If you have been there, you will know roughly what I mean. I say 'roughly' because no two panic disorders are exactly the same. I was lucky, that March day. My body finally broke through and forced me to listen. I say 'finally' because, long months before, a still, small voice had been trying to catch my attention, to alert me that something was hurting. The proof is in the poem I had written then. I called it 'Cacophonies'.

O the street was windswept and noisy
And he loved it.
The traffic was brawling and fractious,
And he found it musical.
The shops were dens of agitation, loudspeakers blared at him,
Tills made their worried, neurotic notation
of squeaks and whimpers
when they ran up amounts,
But he revelled
In their busyness, their bluster.

He went home through sirens blaring, horns bleating,
Brakes squealing and the radio playing
Till he won to the placid quietness of a room
Overlooking the garden.
And there in a chair
He slumped and attuned his hearing
For the first time, in the limpid stillness
Of late afternoon,
To the sobbing of his heart within him,
Louder than alarms.

Russell Hogan once asked if there could be any doubt that our bodies are constantly trying to communicate with us.

You say to your head: 'We're going to that party tonight, and we're going to smile, and talk to all these people we don't want to smile or talk to.' Your head says: 'Ache, ache, ache.' You say to your gall bladder: 'I'm so bitter, life is so hard.' Your gall bladder says: 'If you feel that way about it, I'll commemorate it with a stone.' Your heart says: 'I'm so heavy. I have no ease. You are doing things with only half of me. You are not doing what is close to me. You're following a path without me. I am not in good self. I have no self for what you are doing. You are not going to the "me" of the matter. Maybe I'll attack you.' If your heart says that to you, then you'll listen because by then you're probably getting pains down your left arm. And let's hope your emergency department isn't on strike.

Language, 24 hours a day, 1,440 minutes daily, 86,400 seconds from dawn to dusk – our bodies are talking to us. And that was hard to accept. My pride for a while was blistered and sore. I had lost an image of myself that I had grown very fond of, the image of one who coped, one who could tough out the slings and arrows of outrageous fortune. I was a survivor, I thought.

The day I let go of my anger at being ill was the day I started to get better. 'You need an asylum,' said the doctor, 'a place of safety.' I must have looked startled, because he went on quickly to describe what he meant. 'Not being you, for a while', he said – 'the public you.'

As it happens, we live in a manse where the back door faces the street, and the front door opens out into a vast garden surrounded by hedges. The asylum was at hand. Here was a private territory where I could be everything my public life forbade: dirty, dishevelled, lazy, impulsive, distracted by minor tasks, mindless. Knowing I had hours and hours to fill, I made small tasks into day-long diversions. There were no deadlines to meet here. It was like reading a good book; you dawdle over each page because you don't want the story to end.

My colleague loaned me a copy of *Gladiator*, the film about a demoted general in the Roman army who had to learn how to survive in the heat and dust of the arena. Ah, tread softly here, for you tread upon my coincidences. I watched the video time and again. I noticed how Maximus, played by Russell Crowe, bends down to rub sand into his palms before going into the amphitheatre, the better to secure the grip on his sword. I bent down and gathered handfuls of Perth's soil, and rubbed them into my hands, the better to secure my grasp of the spade, the hoe, the rake and the shears.

Looking back now, I notice three things. Being a crofter's son, I grew up with no experience of gardens. Men who work the land all day don't rush home at night to plant, or weed, or trim lawns. To adapt a Billy Connolly phrase, to them it's like washing a hankie. A garden, to them, is not a place of retreat. For me, though, last spring, our patch of ground, hidden away from the street, was definitely a bolt hole. I think I began to see it as the croft I had known as a boy, in miniature. My wife jokes about the way I gather up grass clippings into little heaps. 'Ah, back on the croft, are we?' she says. Yes, last April, May, June and July I went back to the croft; I walked my little acres, shaped my tiny fields, hefted stones, built fences, cut timber. I went back to the safe place, which is childhood.

And there is the powerful vibration in the fingers as they curl round the shaft of the hoe my father gave me years and years ago. The wood carries the invisible stamp of his sweat. Who is to say I was not linking hands with him when I picked up my tools of a morning? There was some communion there between us. The spirit level, which was my grandfather's, has come down to me: his initials are stamped on it ... a skilled carpenter, he made things. Who is to say his gifts were not present to me when I sought a level?

And thirdly, my habit of rubbing loose earth on to my palms in the manner of a gladiator tells me now that I regarded this immersion in gardening as being more to do with combat than communion with the world of growing things. A fight. Not a fight with the weeds and couch-grass and dandelions only, but the battle inside me, the need to regain lost ground, the struggle to get away from the horrific sensation of weightlessness which had forced me to retreat from a service of Holy Communion in March, dizzy and disorientated. Quite literally, I was needing to be earthed again – and, day after day, I anointed my hands with the rough, grainy stuff of existence.

The way I worked was totally uncoordinated. I flitted from task to task with sublime unconcern. The decision not to decide on something is of course a decision in itself. I made scores of them. 'Will I do this now?' 'No, I'll do it later.' 'How much later?' 'Does it matter?' 'No. OK.'

Six weeks into my illness, I was writing letters to our daughter Ruth in Belfast *à la* Bridget Jones.

Saturday May 12
Potatoes through ground: 7 (very good). Onions weeded. Border not weeded (very bad). Path under control (nearly).
Grass not cut. Very bad. Onions awful to weed. Was bent over for an hour. Could not straighten up when had to answer door-

bell. Visitor took one look and fled. Border still in state of chaos. Chased off three cats with foul curses. Grass out of control.

Sunday May 13

Potatoes through: 10 Excellent. Onions: no change. Parsley attacked by birds: very angry. Grass not cut: old girl frowning a bit. Border: tinkered with fork for 3 minutes. Gave up in despair.

Monday May 14

Grass: leopards and panthers could hide in swaying fronds. Old girl very tight-lipped.

Potatoes 17, brill; onions, stout chaps; grass – herd of zebra and an elephant or two barely able to be detected in lush verdure!

Tuesday May 15

Potatoes 27, very good, grass now threatening to obscure view of Perth. Have begun to trim edges of lawn but this involves much bending over and cannot seem to straighten up again. Jehovah's Witness came to door and told me where to find truth. Could not be sure if he meant it as I was looking at his shoes at the time.

Beneath the humour of these observations lies the comfortable truth that the garden was on the rampage. I was discovering that a garden rewards you for what you do, and it punishes you for what you don't do.

Day after day, the post brought cards and letters. It was like having a continuous birthday. And people came to see me, and I found out an awful lot about visiting, or rather about being visited. Charles Causley has a brilliant poem in which he describes various types of hospital visitor: the one who is all smiles and offers ferocious goodwill; the one who is just miserable; another who blethers on about how the garden is doing and the slates which fell off the roof; another who is long-faced; another who jokes all the time; a fifth who is uncomfortable in the hospital. The sixth visitor is someone who does not say much, brings neither grapes nor chocolates, but has some clean washing which he quietly places in the locker and does not stay the whole hour!

I think we can pause there. Causley's point is made: maybe one visitor in six gets it right. It would be unfair to say that my experience was the same.

Let me just note, in passing, that I found out one or two things from the kind people who called on me. The question 'How are you?' is totally unanswerable. The lady who called once a month and never rang the bell but left a magazine and a bag of toffees on the doorstep is a genius. The man who dropped in twice to ask if I wanted to go on a long car-trip with him, to get me out of my exile, was also a genius because he took it for granted that I did not want to talk about what was wrong with me. The unexpected visit can be a lovely surprise, but the unexpected invitation is sometimes a surprise too far. One day, Rosemary, looking as ever like something out of *Vogue*, walks down the garden and ambushes me in the onion patch with the blithe assertion: 'I'm taking you to lunch!' 'No, you're not', I had to say. She is a good friend, and she took my refusal with grace and good humour. Some callers popped in for ten minutes, so they said, and stayed for an hour. They could not have known how exhausted I was at the end of such a visit. Some days, I put a sign on the door saying: 'Dear friends, please do not call today.' It is amazing how many people develop blindness when they are determined to do you good. Some visitors said, at the door: 'Are you in? I'll go away if you're not.' Bless them. One staunch friend offered to come and be the dragon at the gate, defending me against all comers. And so she did, and I thank her mightily.

And I thank too, now, the people who were repulsed and accepted that cheerfully. Bless them too.

There were moments of real comedy. One day, the plumber had come to deal with a blocked sink. I had officiated at this chap's wedding many years ago, so we knew each other. Crouching down beneath the offending appliance, he asked me conversationally why I wasn't at work. I told him I was off with exhaustion. He stopped what he was doing, and said in tones of mock disbelief: 'A minister, exhausted? I've never heard of that before!'

What struck me shortly was that there were those who were quick to find a name for my condition, and those who shied away from categorizing. Finlay and Fiona, our sometime best man and his wife, who now live in Wester Ross, came to see us, not long into my illness. 'What's wrong with you?' Finlay said. 'I can't put a name on it', I replied. 'That's fine', he said, 'Maybe it doesn't need to have a name.' And yet some good folk assumed that I was suffering from depression. Some called up the vague and convenient ogre of stress. One day, in despair, I asked my excellent doctor if he thought I was going through a breakdown. 'No', he replied. 'Put it like this', he went on. 'Even a Rolls-Royce has a puncture from time to time.' The kindness in that remark was lost on me at the time, but I realize now how invigorating it is to be placed in the same category as a Roller, and how reassuring it is to be told that you're alright, that the back axle isn't broken and the engine hasn't seized up.

Our daughter Ruth has taught me many Belfast expressions. One of my favourites is the phrase that people say to put others at their ease: 'You're alright.' Stumble over someone's feet on the bus, spill tea in a saucer, knock an elbow in the queue, and someone will say: 'You're alright.' It's a healing little phrase.

During that spring of bitter realism, I had people telling me that I was alright. My wife Meg had a wedding to plan in July. There were trips to Edinburgh, kitchen-table summits, telephone conferences. I felt distanced from it all. Never once did Meg lose her balance. She knew I was not onside in a proper way, so she handled the whole burden of the preparations, but handed me little goals to achieve. 'Go and book rooms in a B&B for Granny and Jennifer'. We live in B&B land, so I thought this would be a doddle. I knocked on doors and rang bells until my knuckles smarted. 'Sorry,' they all said, 'we've been booked up for a year for the All Scotland Jehovah's Witnesses Convention.' In the end, we got them into a hotel.

And my daughters sent me jokes off the Internet, which I cannot repeat in polite society. But they made me laugh. I have them in a folder. I have kept all the cards and letters people sent, because some of them were so brilliant. One lady scribbled on a card: 'Make the most of your time out. Forget about us. Enjoy.' Wonderful!

A Strange Place (2)

There's a phrase of Leonard Cohen's which followed me through Lent about how it is the crack in everything that lets the light in. I had quoted it in a friend's church at an evening service on Ash Wednesday, and I had tried to say something about Lent being a time when the spring days get longer, and the light expands and frees us from the dead of winter. I had asked the congregation of St John's Episcopal Church in Perth if we were ready for this Lent, ready for new shafts of light to be shed on our separate and common journeys. How did you let in the light? Then, in the service, the rector, Bob Fyfe, had marked my forehead with the ashes and said to me: 'Remember that you are dust, and to dust you shall return. Turn away from sin and be faithful to Christ.' Thus was my Lent begun. It ended for me, adrift in the large garden of our manse, hiding, cut off from Easter Day on the greatest day in the Church's life, the day that lifts up the heart like no other, the day that sweeps away the dead hand of Golgotha. It was the first Easter I had missed in 30 years.

We let Easter swamp us in the ancient Church of St John's. It's a day for glorious flowers and white robes and words that shine and sparkle: 'This is the chosen and holy day, the one King and Lord of Sabbaths, the Feast of Feasts and the Triumph of Triumphs.' And, on this Easter Day, I did not have the mental energy to utter these words to myself. There is, in illness, a hellish ability to separate you from the things that matter to you: you feel stranded on an alien shore. One person sent me a door into the locked room where the Risen Christ was out of reach: a meditation she had written. It was startling in its freshness and its vividness. Here is how it began.

How did He feel, that third day, rousing from a different kind of sleep? Did he wake with a start, confused and unsure of where He was? Or was it a gentle coming to, a pleasant sensation, a feeling of peace? Did He cry out with pleasure feeling the stones under His feet, back on solid ground? But it was dark in that cave. How He longed to see the sunlight again, breathe fresh air, fill His lungs with it, until they were full to bursting. This could not be right, shut in this dead man's resting-place. It was a large stone covering the entrance, too big for an ordinary man to move. Did He smile as He made it roll away? Stones were no match for His power. At last, the sun, newly-born itself, flooded His soul, its warmth encompassed his cold body, its rays caused Him to shine.

Carleen, when she worked in St John's a full ten years ago as an assistant minister, had the courage then to do things that I flinched from. Here was an Easter meditation taking the hearer into the tomb of Jesus, leading the listener out into the daylight. It was all so tactile. Darkness and stones and sunshine.

I said to my doctor one day that one of the worst things about my condition was that I had become self-absorbed. His response was quick and blunt. 'Weren't you always?' he said. Ouch. I was very lucky, I had a non-judgemental doctor who nevertheless did not let me off with anything. He supported me and he resisted me. The first time I saw him, I made an utter fool of myself. We had talked for maybe fifteen minutes or so, and I looked at my watch and said that I must be going. He looked at me with a sardonic smile. 'Why?' he asked. 'You have other people to see,' I said. 'Yes?' he said. 'They will be seen, never fear.' I realized that I was in a graceless position. Here was a man giving me of himself, and I was trying to tell him how to do it. Such well-meant arrogance on my part. I suppose I realized that day that I had become a receiver.

We are all of us, from childhood on, urged to be givers. Our Christian take on 'joy' is, famously, the Sunday-school maxim that joy stands for JESUS, OTHERS, YOURSELF … J.O.Y. But we should be taught also how to receive. At the very start of my illness, Donald, a psychiatrist friend, urged me to see this experience as a time to be receptive to new insights into life: a time for reflection, a learning curve. Certainly for someone like myself, who has lived too long, maybe, inside his head, the early summer of 2001 was very tactile. The day really kicks off when you wash your face – and, day after day, I reached my fingers up to touch the skin on my cheeks *as if I did not really expect to find warm flesh there.* I had lost my face. It felt to me like parchment on which someone had scribbled the message 'gone away'. Then, after breakfast (which was part of the learning curve, because I had given up breakfast years before), I went to the toolshed and picked out rakes and forks and the old hoe from the croft. Then it was time for the Maximus moment, when I scooped up a little earth and rubbed it into my palms, and then I attacked the border. I could never have filled that patch of ground without the Machiavellian genius of Iain Brown. Iain has a dream of world domination through horticulture. He grows things like a man possessed, and last year he recruited his wife to inflict seedlings on me. And plants. Not by the dozen, by the hundreds. It felt like being in the Latin classroom again. She would come staggering down the path with boxes and tubs and pots and containers. 'What is this?' I would groan. 'Lobelias' she would say, with an evil smile. 'And this,' gloating more than Midas with a tax rebate, she would say, 'Cineraria.' And she brought hostas and petunias and begonias and impatiens and dahlias and chrysanthemums and sweet peas, which was great because I can pronounce sweet peas. The Livingstone daisies took me about three days to plant out. I began muttering feebly stuff about not depleting Iain's potting shed, but that only made her cackle with malevolent glee. 'Don't worry,' she would say, 'there's lots more where that came from.' 'That's what I thought you would say', I would groan. By August, the border was aflame with colour.

I had learned a lot from my fingertips. By September, I had also learned how to sit down at a keyboard (but that's another story) – and the poem, which I composed straight to screen, was truly a major breakthrough. For all happy, well-balanced people who do not have a computer, Verdana is a typeface.

So this is how it feels to be in Verdana
now that autumn is here and Mother Nature begins to take off

her make-up and her fancy green frills
(she's tired of performing in public)
my fingertips tell me a
story in lower case.
All summer long, I have listened to their jangled music,
their blunt messages, their blow-by-blow accounts
of what was happening to me.
First, in March, on my birthday,
leaning on the Holy Table for support,
then the long weeks when spades and hoes were all
that fastened me to a purpose: that, and the slender stems
of tiny flowers so much at my mercy
and me at the mercy of them. Their littleness,
beggars at the gates of earth, was a mirror to me.

July was a story in which the punch-lines began to arrive.
The border I had doodled in began to flesh out its true shape.
The sweet peas exploded insistently.
As the August days ended, my fingers went back to school,
and enrolled in this new universe of signs
and encrypted mysteries.

My Lent that year began with a priest's fingertips on my forehead: the imposition of ashes. As the summer ended, I began to feel
that I had learned what it means to engage with life again and with
the senses and the brain and the heart in a better balance. Orthodox Christians have long understood this balance. When they cross
themselves, touching their forehead, their breast and their shoulders,
they are offering up to God the energy of their minds, the fervour of
their hearts and the strength of their arms. It's a powerful reminder,
too, that God loves us body and soul.

I think, if I had a mission statement of my own, it would be John
D. MacDonald's advice that we should sniff the breeze and hug the
kids. I've never had any hesitation about hugging children, because
little girls under the age of two find me quite attractive in a certain
light. But hugging adults has always been more problematic. I have
always been awkward about that – mainly, I think, because I am

Scottish and therefore a bit wary of being too familiar. As my unease and dis-ease waned, however, I learned to hug, however New Age and corny that sounds.

I met a lady in the street, and she looked very down. I asked her if she was having a bad day. She nodded. Before I had made the decision with my head to do so, I put my arms around her and patted her on the back. There is another breakthrough in that simple act. Learning to forsake words, words, words. We use far too many words. When I went back to work, the habit of writing prayers had to be rediscovered. When I did a word-count with this marvellous machine, I noted with delight that the total amount of words in the first prayer I put together was 173. Anything under 200 is crisp.

On the wall of my study is a poem by William Neill. It ends saying that prayers have grown too long, too clever. The word 'clever' haunted me until last summer. It's hard to explain, but the need to *appear* clever has never really bothered me. The need, though, to meet what I considered to be my own standards has always been a whip. Take the subject of prayers, which William Neill refers to. As someone who has given over Saturday nights to writing prayers and sermons for 30 years, I have lived with the question: 'Where do prayers come from?' From books, from recognized masters of the art and craft of speaking compellingly for others to God? From your head? If so, your head will direct you to the books: to the age-old, beautiful, dated, polished gems of devotion from eras long removed from where we live today. From your heart? If so, you will try to make the prayer reflect where you are on your journey. You will salt it with honesty and sweeten it with as much poetry as you dare: the last thing you want is a prayer reeking of the midnight oil, but the second-last thing you want is a sloppy, slipshod piece of tired prose that doesn't catch a little fire or kindle just a tiny spark in the imagination of the people praying with you. There is the sting: to pray with any force or focus, you almost have to try to *be* the people you are speaking for … if only for four minutes or five minutes. In public. In private, sitting at a desk, that leap into the quandaries, regrets, anxieties and dreads of other people can take hours to assay.

What language shall I borrow?
What frame of reference am I using?
What assumptions must I dare not make?
What effect am I striving for?
Who is saying this: the 'I' that is for me? Or the 'I' that is for others?
Where do prayers come from? The foot of the Cross, or the door of the empty tomb?

I suppose these questions tormented me. What also sabotaged my peace of mind on Saturday nights was the feeling that getting it right was not about being clever but about being true to as many people as possible. I wanted what I said to be perfect, in the strict dictionary meaning of the term: *done thoroughly*. 'Forget your perfect offering', sings Leonard Cohen. But I had not been listening – until last year, in March, when I entered that white-out of the spirit in which I lost my bearings and I fell into an abyss which I had dug for myself. Kahlil Gibran says:

> Much of your pain is self-chosen. It is the bitter potion by which the physician in you heals your sick self. Therefore trust the physician, and drink his remedy in silence and tranquillity: For his hand, though heavy and hard, is guided by the tender hand of the Unseen, and the cup he brings, though it burns your lips, has been fashioned of the clay which the Potter has moistened with his own sacred tears.

Climbing out of the abyss has meant, for me, learning to like not being perfect.

> 'There is a crack in everything
> That's how the light gets in.'

It was my great good fortune to have fallen ill in 2001. For a lot of reasons, maybe the chief one was that my colleague swept into the empty space I vacated like a tornado made of zephyrs, one of the meanings of that lovely word being 'anything very fine of its kind'. She can be warm and breezy, and she can be steely when she chooses. Never for a second did I worry about the good health of the church I had abdicated from: I knew it was in excellent hands. On a personal level, not a professional one, I was introduced to the side of me that needed healing: the side I had contrived to deny existed. The stern and steadfast desire to do things thoroughly (the quest for perfection I mentioned earlier) is on the surface laudable. Sitting up until 2am writing a funeral service; hunting the attics of the mind for new ways of doing Christmas, as if the Lord's appearing was a jaded dish for which one has constantly to devise fresh, appetizing sauces; rising to levels of acute concentration when sitting with souls in pain and often bodies in pain; being ready at all times to reprioritize. For this is a life, this ministry of Word and Sacrament, in which the next phone-call can change your entire week. All this looks worthy, but it has a shadow side. It speaks of someone trying just a bit too hard to please everyone. 'Woe to you when all men speak well of you,' says Jesus. But I had not been listening to Him either.

The desire to please everyone is on the surface laudable. Inside my worthy creed, there was the fatal flaw: pleasing others means not pleasing yourself, and sooner or later a lost child in you wails in distress that you have all the candy-wrappers and none of the candy. The lost child broke through in March 2001, which forced me to go looking for the found child in the garden planting Maris Pipers and sweet peas and building little dykes with old paving stones. And I began to recognize him again, very gradually. My face came back too, that papery mask which I had 'begun to doubt'. It began to feel like it belonged to me again.

Not long after I was gifted access to a keyboard, I tapped out one evening a wee list of notes to myself. I called them 'The Paroxetine Paradoxes', Paroxetine being the name of the medication I was given. One reads: 'When I disappeared i.e. dropped out, I discarded all my public selves. I became visible again.' It is true. I had vanished into the things I did. Another note to self: 'I had a face for everyone before. Now I have reclaimed it. It is no longer for hire.'

The Prodigal Son, says Jesus, 'came to himself'. And then he heads for home. That set of three words contains a library of insight. What a long way the Prodigal has to go before that coming-to-himself opens his eyes and unclenches his pride. What a learning curve. I'm ready now to admit that pride had sunk its talons into me: pride in my blind attempt to do and be and speak and pray so ceaselessly that it looked effortless, so thoroughly that it was perfect. *Forget your perfect offering.* It can become a golden calf you bow down to.

One last word which churns my stomach to confess. Before I was ill, I extended sympathy and understanding to people who were sidelined with symptoms like mine. Sympathy with a small 's'. Understanding with a small 'u'. Part of me felt that I was superior to them, because I was a survivor. There – it is said. It was excised, that arrogance, in the spring of 2001. In the best and sweetest sense of the word, I had finally begun to listen to my own saint, John the Baptist. 'Repent', he said.

A Strange Place (3)

A short story by James Kelman begins with the patient entering the doctor's consulting room, aghast at himself for calling the doctor 'Sir'. Why has he said that, he wonders? Why has he wrong-footed himself? I wrong-footed myself on my first visit to the doctor by trying to cut short the conversation we were having. But, as the spring became summer, our fortnightly meetings meant more and more to me: sitting in the waiting room felt as safe to me as standing on a ledge of a building three storeys up from the street. Five yards away, sitting at the doctor's desk, I was back on solid ground.

He always walked *with* me to his room – never in front. That may seem trivial; to me, it was immense. All notions of the minister being a leader flounder on the rock of how much it matters to the minister to be seen as being out in front – that is, does it feed his or her ego? Far better to be a companion, one who walks beside.

And there are times when we ministers would do well to be openly baffled. Petru Dumitriu contrasts the one he calls a devil-theologian who forgets to be humble and admits he doesn't know and should be silent, and the devil-preacher who talks and talks about God until God gives up his emptied heart – the devil-preacher who possesses those who preach to others instead of praying in silence. (So, is preaching forbidden? Certainly not – but one must humiliate, humble oneself before, during and after, and take refuge as soon as possible in prayer, one-to-one with God, instead of making some self-important public monologue.) Ah, Dumitriu, you are so right and you are also wrong. What do you do when this activity of prayer, one-to-one with God, becomes some self-important, *private* monologue? Sometimes, in a fantasy I have, I think that the only Gospel story which Divinity students should be forced to study for a year is the Temptation in the wilderness. 'Save Your energy,' says the tempter to Jesus, 'Save Yourself.' He chose to give away the love, to feed the energies of grace and healing into the lives of others. He chose relationship.

Ted Loder's way with language is not always easy. In one of his prayers, he describes salvation as 'communal' – the *ours* of beauty, truth, hope, the *we* of mercy, wholeness, atonement, the *together* of wolves and lambs and all reunion, the *us* of wedding feasts, Samaritans, prodigals, and every occasion of rejoicing: the love that is, and never ends, being relational, the meeting, the surprise of connection. When I eventually got back to taking services again, I said a different benediction: 'The blessing of the Father, the Son and the Holy Spirit be with *us*.' The ours, the we, the us that Ted speaks about.

Sometimes, in our desire to be at one with others, we assure them that we know exactly what they are going through. People would say this to me, and I realized that they were probably selling their own experience short. I wanted to say to them that their abyss was maybe twice as unbearable as mine, because at no time did I ever spend a whole day under the duvet or staring at the wall. I was lucky. Panic attacks are awful, but they did not paralyze me. So, I made a promise to myself that I would never say to anyone: 'I know exactly what you're going through' – because I don't.

The fables of Aesop are well known; the fables of Robert Louis Stevenson deserve to be better known. I love the one called *The Tadpole and the Frog*. 'Be ashamed of yourself,' said the frog. 'When I was a tadpole, I had no tail.' 'Just what I thought!' said the frog. 'You never were a tadpole.' Point taken. Speak of what you know, and don't try to be someone else.

Being all things to all men is a delicate balancing act. I think I overdid it. John Berger says that the desire to proliferate the self into many selves may initially grow from a tendency to exhibitionism. And sadly, the minister is constantly being invited to be an exhibitionist.

At summer's end, my doctor handed me over to a psychiatrist. I felt deprived and bereft. The rapport we had built up was too good to relinquish, and that says a lot more about him than it says about me. The word 'psychiatrist' means 'a doctor of the soul'. I went to our first session with fear and foreboding: what would he want to know? What would I want to disclose, and what would I want to withhold? I made a promise to myself: I would try to be honest and I would try not to be an exhibitionist, so I would not play word-games with him. I cannot do crosswords, but I can do word-games. The man who was dealing with me was alert to the problem we were facing, because we knew each other. He said to me at our first session: 'You may well hate me when this is over.' I said: 'OK.'

We fear those who may be able to heal us. They ask us to give them access to the murky corners of our history where our self-loathing writhes and gesticulates. They ask us to face the bits of ourselves we have tried to throw a veil over. They ask us to trust them with the masks we have grown to rely on. In the operating theatre, we surrender to the surgeon; in the context of the psychiatrist's office, there is no anaesthetic. Acceptance is the only currency here.

Along with the one-to-one encounter with the psychiatrist came my awakening to the world of keyboards, desktops, icons and files. I had written myself off completely in the area of computer wizardry, but Iain Brown (he of the lobelias and begonias and cineraria and so on) had written to me to offer me a machine *and* instruction if only I would give him the word. 'Half an hour's notice is all I need', he said. I ignored the siren voice of such an offer: he was opening doors I was scared of. Why? The fear of being proved totally stupid, that's why. Machinery and I have always enjoyed a fraught relationship: I cannot fix cars that break down, cigarette-lighters develop inex-plicable faults in my keeping, and when we got our video-recorder my daughters had to remind me gently that you have to put a video cassette into the thing if you want to record something. Quite sim-ply, I have techno-fear – and here was the expert who was willing to give me of himself at a computer screen. Three men all reinforcing a prickly truth: you have to move on, boy. And you have to bite down on your embarrassment at needing help to do so.

Had someone told me in March, before I lurched out of the chapel to drink strong tea in the vestry, that I needed help, I would have bitten their head off. I would have been insulted. I, who fondly hoped that I had mastered humility, had in fact a monstrous and quite manic ego. To recognize that now is like being left off the leash to run and frolic at will. What was I to do with this fumbling new repertoire of skills which the keyboard was offering? It took me half an hour to type a page – but, for a scribbler, as I am, the thrill of seeing words appear in front of your eyes is an electric experience. The computer is my new consoler. It's a magic thing. I sit in front of it like most people sit in front of their television sets.

'It's only a glorified typewriter,' my son-in-law once told me. But he isn't a writer. He doesn't know what it is when words bite into space, flash into light, when the thoughts that come into the head can be followed at once by words, which encourage more thoughts and more words to follow. With a typewriter, it's like walking through mud. With a computer, it's ice-skating. It's a blazing blast, it's one run for the fun, the glory and the escape.

I wrote a book. In Scots. It's about my first year as a student in Aberdeen in 1963, about failing exams and being demoted from Honours Classics and various other crises like narrowly avoiding arrest one evening for impersonating a friend. The psychiatrist could not contain his glee when I told him what I was writing. 'The book is about you, now,' he said. 'You are telling the story of these last few months.' 'Tosh,' I said. 'I've wanted to write this book for years.' 'So, why now?' he asked. 'Because,' I answered with a sigh (some things are not obvious, even to psychiatrists), 'I have the time and I have the machine.' Even a child could see that. But the man sitting at his desk three feet away is a very shrewd and observant cookie. 'Put it like this,' he said. 'You go to university in 1963 with quite a lot of expectations hovering around you. You have done well at school in Latin and Greek, and your teachers are bound to be looking for a similar performance at Aberdeen. It's a small world, the world of Classics. You are being watched. You do not fulfil the expectations of your mentors. You are demoted, as you say.' A mental image of myself in the manse garden, rubbing earth into my hands (the Maximus moment), flits across my mind. 'This year has been, for you,' he goes on, 'a throwback to 1963. You have had to stop work with nervous exhaustion, and that may feel to you like a failure of some sort, a failure to meet the expectations of others. Maybe you feel that you have not met your own expectations of yourself. The book is as much about 2001 as it is about 1963.' I shrugged my shoulders.

'Has it got a title?' he asked. I told him: '*Thalassa, Thalassa*.' 'You'll have to explain that,' he grinned. 'My Latin is a bit rusty.' 'It's Greek,' I said. 'It means "The sea, the sea!" It's what the army of mercenaries shouted when they won through, after a horrific march in winter through hostile territory, to a point where they could see, far off, the waters of the Black Sea. The sea represented to them the hope of getting home again after their hardships and ...' The psychiatrist was chuckling by now. 'Listen to yourself,' he said. 'You couldn't, maybe, be talking about coming to a point where you can see the way forward now, a possibility of setting sail again?' I glowered at him with unconcealed dismay. 'See you next week,' he said, happy as a sandboy.

The Greek army marchin tae safety, land-locked an weary, herriet on ilka side, cam at last tae a vantage-pint faar they could see, far aff, the braid glint o the Black Sea. The roar fae a thoosan throats gaed up, fae strategoi an taxiarchoi an lochagoi and stratiotai alike: a cry o relief an waalcome; aa o a sudden their howps o hamecomin bleezed again intill an eident lowe.

Thalassa! Thalassa!
The sea! The sea!

The book ends in September 1964, but that is only partly true. I added on a 'postlude', a story written from the perspective of one of the foot-soldiers in Cyrus's fleeing army. He speaks about mutiny in the ranks, deserters, the biting cold, the danger they were in from the tribesmen of the hill-country, the young lieutenant who goaded them on and kept an iron grip on discipline. One of the foot-soldiers. Maybe that's where my long march has taken me.

'Tak your share of drees', says Paul to Timothy, in the Lorimer translation, 'like a guid sodger o Christ Jesus.' 'Take your share of suffering as a good soldier of Christ Jesus.'

But it is still a long march under Your flag, Lord, and the terrain is hostile. We wake up each day hoping that this bit will be easier –

and it rarely is. The hills do not get less steep; and the ravines lurk in wait for the false step, the lurch into the abyss. We cannot see where we are heading half the time. The mist comes down and we lose our sense of direction. We are so far from home. The snow freezes more than hands and feet and fingers, it freezes the heart. The wind in our faces cuts like a knife.

Progress is slow: we wade in the gullies and the howes with feet that no longer belong to us, they are so numb. And as for those we march with! They are out of step half the time, they hold us back, they quarrel and girn, and each one thinks the bit of the regiment *they* belong to is the only bit that matters. They boast and swagger, some of them, that they are the backbone of the whole force. Call these Cretans bowmen? They couldn't hit a barn door at 20 paces. Where did this ragtag-and-bobtail bunch of misfits come from? Some of them quit and slink away: good riddance to them. I wonder sometimes why I ever enlisted. What are we fighting for? Land and possessions? Glory and honour? Or mere survival?

'Enlarge our hearts,' says George MacLeod, 'to serve all Christians with uncalculating love: without waiting: even should they spurn us or turn from us.' The enlarged heart is one of the trophies I take with me from the battlefield of the year 2001: the understanding that many people are quietly engaged in their own desperate struggle to get through the days. Not long after I had gone off sick, the phone rang, and it was a young friend I had not heard from for ages. He asked after me, and then I asked about him. Two minutes into his frank recital of the vice he was squeezed in, I was shouting at him to go and see his doctor. It was my illness that gave him the courage to phone me and tell me where he was pinned. Thereafter we wrote and exchanged notes all though the summer – but I know that if I had not entered the abyss, he would not have felt able to pick up the phone and tell me about himself.

It was my great good fortune to have fallen ill in the spring and summer of that year. Had I not done so, I would not have met some other people in the same strange place – and I would not have met myself.

An Iona Pilgrimage

A meditative journey round the island

When the Religious Broadcasting Department of BBC Scotland dis-
covered that David Ogston had never visited Iona, a radio producer
who knew the island well took him there to record the effect on him
of the island, which George MacLeod, the founder of the Iona Com-
munity, liked to call 'a very thin place, where only a piece of tissue
paper separates heaven and earth, the sacred and the secular'.

They've been here before, these pilgrims walking up the jetty from
the boat: they trust the stores to be in their appointed places and
the landmarks to be solidly, exactly, where their memories left
them. Young people with the burden of their travels on their backs,
the Swedish rucksack, a German tent, fishing gear, the axes for
the archaeologists, the knapsack with the sandwiches, the rolled-
up groundsheet: yes, and the spare boots and the red socks that
were almost forgotten at the last campsite and were snatched from
a drying line as an afterthought. And they do not talk, for they are
glancing now to the left and now to the right, trying to drink in
what it means to be a dancer who has been invested with light-
ness, invested with a history, made heirs apparent of an atmosphere
which is created daily by the pilgrim feet of those who come here as
if in answer to a summons.

* * *

The horse that is pulling us is called Khan, as in Genghis. We are
approaching the Abbey by the way of the high road, along the dykes
which are built of this fabulous russet-brown mottled stone. There
are two ways to the Abbey on Iona: you can take the high road,

which is what we're doing, or you can take the low road, which is along the machair beside the sea – and somehow, although the high road is clear and broad and easy, it's the low road which is interesting, because as you come to the Abbey, you get the feeling that you're creeping up on it and surprising it a bit. Genghis must be going at about three miles an hour, which is the right speed for Iona; in fact, maybe he's going slightly less than three miles an hour.

* * *

The Abbey is a marvellous mixture of lines and silhouettes and sharpness which are all offset by the gentleness of what is in front of you as you approach it. There is a superb piece of well-tended grass, there's a garden, then there's this rough outcrop of rock which is face-on to the Abbey, very much as if it were in confrontation with this sculptured and shaped and ordered reality. The building itself is angled towards the Sound of Iona, so in a strange sort of way the Abbey seems to be almost floating on the surface of the water. I suppose that makes me imagine that this is a great ship ready for voyages and ready to go exploring.

* * *

There is tremendous order and neatness and evidence of all the work that's gone into this place since George MacLeod and a small group of men came here in 1938 to make these ruins a living centre of witness and faith again. As I come through the door, I think what strikes me first is the feeling of space, which is enhanced at this moment by a bird flying up and down the length of the church. This is a building far too big for 12 or 13 monks – but then, perhaps it's quite a bit bigger than the house that Columba started with. This is where they built the house of prayer. And, as they did so, the hammers and the axes sang in the still clear air of Iona, stones grated on stones, metal rasped on the edges of the boulders and the pebbles and the rocks which they shaped and dressed and levered into place. The rough men of God became exact at creating line and elevation and symmetry and balance. And they discovered by trial and error just what the stresses and the tensions had to be to make this place fast. There was no peace in this great house until it was finished – and then, when it was done, it was anchored to the land here just beneath the shadow of Dun Ì, and they fixed the roof tree, and then the other litanies began.

* * *

'Open our lips, O God' – yes certainly, but I think many people come to the Abbey now, not just to speak or to sing or to declare their certainties or to voice their doubts, but they come here just to absorb this place, just to listen, to take the small step from the arrogance of knowing or the desperation of knowing nothing, to that white silence of a mind which is cleansed of all its clamant convictions and all its clamant questions, and to honour the old Bible text 'Speak, Lord, for thy servant heareth', which we have far too often turned upside down and changed into 'Hear, Lord, for thy servant speaketh'. Listening to God means sometimes being ready to be banished from your motherland of absolutes and leaving every loved familiar highway in order to wait on the God who is always dodging our hard-and-fast descriptions of him, or dancing out of reach just as we think we've captured him and contained him.

* * *

I've walked down the road and through a few gates and across a field to this incredible expanse of white sand called the White Strand of the Monks. The story goes that on Christmas Eve AD 986 the Abbot and 15 of his monks were herded together here by a Danish raiding party and put to the sword. So, this amazingly quiet scene, where the only sound is of waves, is a place of slaughter and a place of death, a place of what the Celts called the 'Red Martyrdom', the giving up of your life, the shedding of your blood for the faith or an ideal or a hope or a dream that you held most dear. The Celts made a distinction between Red Martyrdom and 'White Martyrdom'. The White Martyrdom was not obviously so serious or so exacting as the Red. The White Martyrdom meant giving something up, leaving home or clansmen or familiar loved and dearly held scenes in order perhaps to follow the call of Christ. But here on this beach the Red Martyrdom happened – and, for the monks and the Abbot, perhaps it was the entering into a glory for them, but it certainly brought the glory of sacrifice once again to Iona. At this time of year when we commemorate the dead, we should make a little pilgrimage to places like this which are marked in memory and in legend and in our own experience, and at this time when we surrender the dead to the safe-keeping of Almighty God, it is only right and good that we should remember those who entered the Red Martyrdom: the confessors, martyrs, apostles, prophets, saints of every age and saints of this age. We might say for them the Russian Orthodox prayer of commemor-ation of the dead: 'Give rest, O Christ, to your servants with your saints, where there is no more sorrow, nor sadness, neither sighing nor pain, but life everlasting. Grant that they may be as children of the day that knows no evening, and grant that they may come to the fullness of all their gifts in the eternal kingdom, through Jesus Christ our Lord, Amen.'

If this White Strand of the Monks on the shores of Iona is a place of the Red Martyrdom, I am wondering now if the White Martyrdom happens in every place, where we have to face up to the prospect of giving up, letting go, relinquishing something in order to win some-thing greater. There is a bay on Iona called St Columba's Bay, where the Iona Community take pilgrims and visitors, and they invite them to pick up a pebble from the side of the water. They ask people to see in that small stone something in themselves which they maybe hate or fear, or something which they cling on to, which they could happily and perhaps better live without – and throw that stone out into the sea, symbolically throwing away what they would be bet-ter without. Well, I've come here, down to the very tip of the shore, right to the water's edge. The colours are amazing here, there's green and blue and white shredded into a million dots of light. I've got a stone in my right hand, but I haven't thrown it yet. I can see a boat; there's two birds just to the right of me, but there's a whole flock of gulls sitting, looking and watching and waiting – and I think if I were honest with you I would say I'm waiting too, for some of the vibrations of this place to quieten down inside me so that I can do something deliberate and something quite personal.

* * *

On our way here, I found this cross and this inscription on it: 'To Elizabeth Sutherland wife of George, the eighth Duke of Argyll, this cross is erected by her husband on the island she loved – 1879', and then on the base of the cross there is a memorial to their daughter Victoria, and the date on the base is 1910. What I found just beside the wall that shelters this cross was a young person sleeping, lying on her side, between the cross and the sea, quite oblivious to the world and all the passers-by and quite oblivious to me. Who was the sleeper? Some weary hiker, maybe, or some exhausted pilgrim, some wayfarer who had opted out of Iona for an hour, or half an hour, or ten minutes? For some strange reason, I found myself vaguely annoyed. I'd come here to soak myself in all the signs and the symbols and the atmosphere of a holy place. I'd come to remind myself of a faith that speaks about dying and rising again, and here I'd found somebody who had simply, literally turned their back on all of this. And part of me said: how can you opt out of the suffering of Christ, how can you be at ease when every hour and every minute somewhere someone is picking up that cross and facing up to pain and cruelty, or mockery or harassment or persecution, or suffering; how can you sleep? And then it dawned on me, there's a kind of blithe sublimity in knowing when to let the cross protect you or shelter you or guard you. For Calvary, of all the places on Earth, was exactly where the peace of God was and is and always will become human and placed at our disposal. So, this evening I will say the liturgy which the Iona community has put together for the evening prayer: 'O Son of the tears, of the wounds, of the piercings, may your cross this night be shielding all.'

* * *

This bay is where Columba first set foot on this island. There he was, an Irish monk: he beached his small boat here, and he started dancing. Here's the place that he came to, to serve the terms of his banishment. Columba came here because he had blood to answer for. So, this point on the island is where he began the epic task of rebuilding himself and all the wide waters that separated him from all that he knew and loved and what he'd lost: all these waters baptized him into a life of peace and into a commission.

O Lamb of God that takes away the sin of the world – have mercy on us,
O Lamb of God that takes away the sin of the world – grant us your peace.

Is this where I have come a long way to find that saint that is within me, having met the sinner in me too many times? Out of the mist of legend I can see Columba, standing sick at heart, orphaned from mother Ireland, straining to see the lost familiar shore and seeing nothing of the land he left behind. I can see him. I can see his eyes brimming with tears. I can see the salt wave of his loss and nostalgia washing over him.

* * *

I'm at the top of Dun Ì now, which is the hill above the Abbey – and from here you can see all Iona and all the water circling it. To the north just down below me, the White Strand of the Monks; and then down to the south, the Abbey fills the eye of course. I can see the MacLeod Centre, which was one of the last great building enterprises of the community and which George MacLeod lived to see completed before he died. It's funny to think of George MacLeod in the Communion of the Saints – because he seemed indestructible. But there is a marvellous line in the Folk Communion which George wrote and used in the Abbey, where he says something about Columba and Ninian and Kentigern 'who can't really be dead' – and that's exactly what I would think of George MacLeod now too, that somehow he's not with us but he can't really be dead.

Simply by clambering up here, I've done enough hard work to feel the prickle of sweat all over me. I've certainly stopped dancing.

I may have danced off the ferry, but this hill stops you doing that for at least a wee while. Maybe it's taken a film of sweat all over my face to help me to wipe away the film of fairy dust which it would be so easy to sprinkle on an experience and a place like this. It's too easy to think of Iona as being enchanted, as if the spell and the magic worked at the pressing of a switch or the turning of a lever. But all that sweat has introduced me to the sweat of all those monks who came from Ireland in tiny boats some 1,400 years ago. Then the awesome effort of building a monastery and a chapter house and a nunnery with their bare hands. The sweat I'm feeling has introduced me to the weight of the coffins of the early kings of Scotland as they were carried to their resting place in the shadow of the Abbey. I can sense, and I maybe couldn't do this before, the strength and the energy and the activity and the struggle that has gone into the crofting and the farming and the living here, and that goes on day by day and every passing day.

I can feel the determination and persistence of all those men who set to work here in 1938 to make the Abbey into what it is today. I can sense that all this creative work of studying and interpreting and presenting and representing the Gospel is effort, because the Gospel is not content with mild and polite discipleship, but insists on a wholehearted 'yes' which taxes you and tires you and pushes you beyond yourself and your limits. And maybe being pushed that way is something like the White Martyrdom, leaving your comfortable self, leaving your bland assumptions, leaving your limited and confined point of view in order to risk being in the dance and to risk that the dance will lead you from where you are to where you'd never thought you'd be.

So, up here on Dun Ì, I think we can sing a kingdom into being from wave to wave and base of waterfall, from sea to sea and every river mouth, from the high crags to where the harvest ripens. All that you made shall praise you and praise the majesty of your imagining.

Man, ye were safe

A poem celebrating the risk of the Incarnation

Man, ye were safe i' the biggins o' Bethlehem,
Row't i' the strae far awa' frae the steer;
An' the fowk that were geddert had never a notion
O' fit was yer eerin in a' the mineer.

Fit wis it gaur't ye tae traivel awa' fae't
Trystin' yer cronies awa' frae the sea?
Man, they were snod at their traffic an' tradin'
An winnert b'times cudn' ye latten them be?

An' syne foo they winnert faun traikin ahin' ye
Wi' never a bield nor a bakin' o' breid,
Foo often ye tell't 'em the teuchats abeen them
Pit naething bit sangs i' the mous that they feed.

Man, ye were safe gin ye never had dauchled,
Had wipet Jerusalem's stew fae yer sheen,
Bit na – ye wad gather her fushionless chickens –
O, bit gin only ye'd left her aleen.

Ye left her tae tak' ye, an' Judas took leave
Tae feather his nest on yer tree –
An a' the eleiven that didna tak money
Took wauges o' fear for their fee.

A' the days o' yer breath ye had never a bed
Nor ever a reef o' yer ain –
They gaed ye a cradle fanever ye cam'
An' they gaed ye a lair at the en'.

Man, ye were safe i' the oxter o' God
But ye traivelt the mairches o' sin –
Ye measured the acres o' Heaven amang us,
An' opened the gates o' the Grave to the win'.

This poem starts with how safe Jesus would have been had He stayed in the village of Bethlehem. Why could you not have left Your disciples where they were at home? Why did You stay in dangerous Jerusalem? But Judas 'feathered his nest', and the others were afraid. You had nowhere to rest. Though safe in God's embrace, You chose to open the grave to the wind.

The Disciples' Journey

A meditation on discipleship then and now

Wee Willie Winkie rins throwe the toon,
Up stairs an doon stairs in his nicht goon,
Tirlin at the windae, cryin at the lock,
'Are the weans in their bed, for it's now ten o'clock?'
An the saicint verse?
Ah! Faa kens the saicint verse,
or the third, or the fourth, or the fifth?
Aye, Willie Miller's poem his 5 verses.
Noo: faa needs tae ken that?
I dae, for a start.
It's one o the things I dae on a journey,
recite poems tae masel. If I can mind them.

Or I listen to music, on a journey. It keeps ye oot o langer, as we say.
Or, safe in the privacy of my car, I micht sing a bit –
if I can mind the wirds.

Or I mind on Bible passages,
the passages wi the lowe o poetry in 'em,
wirds that shine an shimmer in yer heid.

'Luve is patientfu;
luve is couthie an kind;
luve is nane jailous;
nane sprosie;
nane bowdent wi pride;
nane mislaired;
nane hame-drauchtit;
nane toustie.'

Noo, wi that laid doon as the feerin:
the furrow that guides the rest:
lat's see faat some did on a journey.

They hid neither music nor sangs tae keep them knypin on. But
Mark says the twists an turns o the road that day gaed in fell quick,
for the men hid an argument. Here's foo he tells it:

They left faar they waar, an gaed on throwe Galilee; withoot lattin
on tae onybody faar they wis heidin for. He wis tryin tae wise His
disciples. He tell't em: the Son o man is bound for capture, an faan
men get a haud o Him they will dee Him tae daith. An efter they
hae killed Him, He will rise come the third day. But they could mak
neither heid nor tail o faat He spak aboot, an they wis feart tae speir.
So they won till Capernaum. Eence they wis aa settled He says till
'em: 'faat wis't ye wis aa sae het up aboot on the wye here?' But
naebody brok breath, because aa the wye tae Capernaum they hid
been nippin een anither aboot faa wis the greatest. An Jesus took a
seat, an gethert the twal disciples roon aboot Him. An He says till
'em: 'Gin ony man ettles tae be foremaist, that very man will hae tae
learn tae be hinmaist, an look efter aabody else.'

Syne He took a bairn, an stood the bairn richt at the hert o the
boorach, an He took the bairn intil His oxter, an said till 'em: 'Faa
welcomes a smout like this in My name welcomes Me: an ony een
that welcomes Me, welcomes nae Me but Him that sent Me.'

Lat's haud up this ae thocht first avaa: that Jesus wis on the same
road as the twal disciples, bit nae sae close up tae them that He kent
faat they wis spikkin aboot as they traivelled – it wisna tull they wis
sattled in their lodgin in Capernaum that He speired them – 'Fit wis't
ye wis aa sae het up aboot on the wye here?'

The question loups up at me, I canna jouk it – foo far fae the
disciples did He walk the road? Wis He ahin them or afore them?
Faat wye did He choose tae traivel aleen? To think His ain thochts?
Tae get awa fae their newsin an speirin an bickerin? Or wis't aa een
o His tests, tae see faat they wid dae if they thocht He wis oot ear-
shot, ower far tae spy on them? Daes it nae mak ye winner again foo
God gies us leave fyles, tae caa forrit wirsels?

32

Saviour an Lord,
You gyang afore us,
You traivel in front o's.
You map the grun we dinna ken,
An there's naewye we gyang
But You hinna been there.

Christ o the desert: there is
Nae temptation You hinna
Faced an focht for's.

Christ o the storm on the face
O the loch: there is
Nae chaos You canna quaeten.

Christ o the brae-face: there is
Nae hunger You canna meet.

Christ o the gairden o Gethsemane:
There is nae loneliness
You hinna tholed.
Christ o the stobs: there is
Nae insult You hinna carried.

Christ o the nails: there is
Nae weird You hinna dree'd.

Christ o risin: You gyang
In front o's tae prepare a place
For's, so that faar You are,
We micht be anaa.

Gin we gyang up tae heiven,
You are there.

Gin we mak oor bed in daith,
Again we find Ye.

So: richtly, gledly, blithely,
We proclaim You,
Risen Lord
Christ afore us.
But here: here, Lord: on the wye
Tae Capernaum,
I jaloose Ye were ahint
The Twal.
I hear Ye tell em,
Caa forrit, lads,
Gie me some space.
I hear them, contermashious chiels,
Come back, at Ye –
Bide wi's, Jesus,
We're weariet withoot Ye.
Bit Ye wid hae neen o't –
Caa forrit, lads, Ye said.

An so they did.
They traivelled athoot Him.
An they fell tae fechtin.

Saviour an Lord,
Is there nae here
A parable for aa Your kirks,
Your Presbyterians,
An Your Catholics,
An Your Baptists,
An Your Episcopalians,
An Your Methodists,
An Your Brethren,
An Your Congregationalists,
An Your Evangelicals,
An Your Liberals,
An Your Pentecostalists,
An Your Traditionalists,
An Your Heich,

An Your Laich,
An Your Radicals,
An Your Aul-fashioned,
An Your Orthodox,
An Your Unorthodox,

That we traivel withoot Ye
At oor peril?
That near twa thoosan eer
Efter Ye were happit
In a spare troch in Bethlehem
We're still fechtin
Aboot faa's the greatest?

Saviour an Lord,
Traivel ahin's
As lang as Ye maun:
But we need You tae
Tae bring us tae book
An tae say tull's fyles:
Faat are ye fechtin aboot?

Traivel ahin's
Catch faat we miss,
Catch faa we miss,
Faan the fishers o men
Get tied up in knots
An forget their nets.

So: noo we're at something fowk cry the sair bit. The moment
o truth. Jesus kens, nae maitter foo far He wis ahin them or afore
them on the road, that they'd fa'en oot wi een enither. Foo daes He
ken that? Because they've brocht the spiled atmosphere o the brattle
wi them inside the hoose; it's sittin on their shooders. It's bleezin in
their een. It's hingin fae their faces. The argument's nae deen wi, nae
feenished. It's jist suspended.

We caa this unfeenished business. Something nae sorted atween man an man, or man an woman, or woman an woman, hings ower their heids like a battle-flag that somebody should hae pulled doon a lang time ago. Something nae sorted pisons ony blitheness we try tae rax for. Something nae sorted gaurs the taste o gweedness tak a wersh an soor quality.

Foo daes Jesus ken? It's in their een.

There's something needin sorted in these men that sit an glower at Him. So He taks a bairn intil His oxter and He says: 'Faaivver taks on this bairn taks me on ...' an we're nae lang or we grasp the shadda side o that – 'Faaivver neglects this bairn ... neglects me ...' I like tae think it wisna the dirl o His wirds aleen that gaured the disciples tak a tummle tae themsels; it wis the sicht o the bairn ana, the bairn in His oxter, that gaed them a begeck.

Faar hid the bairn come fae, aa o a sudden? Wis he magicked up oot a thin air? Wis he hidden awa aneth the table, wytin tae be brocht oot in an emergency? Wis he hine awa, an hid tae be cried on tae come ower tae the Lord for a meenit? Nae neen o these. I wid jaloose the bairn hid been close tee tae them aa aa the time, bit naebody'd noticed him except the Lord Himsel. Tell me I'm wrang – I'm aften wrang – but it seems tae me that the men in that room waar ower teen up wi themsels tae see the little een.

Time an again in the Gospels, Jesus comes throwe as the man that *sees*. He notices faat ithers either dinna see or dinna wint tae see or hinna time tae see. 'The ee', he says, 'is the lamp o the bodie. Gin yer sicht is guid, yer haill bodie will be foo o licht.'

Faat did He see? In a wird, He saa aathing. He couldna walk a dizzen yairds but He fand jewels wytin tae be prized an praised.

'Luik at the birds i the lift: they saw nane, they shear nane, they getherna grain intil barns: an yit your heavenlie Faither gies them their mait. Luik at the wild lilies an the wye they growe: they tchauvna nor spin-na: an yit I tell ye at Solomon himsel in aa his braivitie wisna buskit hauf sae braw.'

He saa fowk. He saa fowk wi promise. Matthew tells us: 'He saw a man caa'd Matthew sittin at his dask an He said til him: "Fallow me ..." an he rase an fallowt Him.'

He saa fowk in pain. He chances upon a funeral. The chief mourner is a widda that his lost her only son. 'Whan Jesus saw the

36

woman, His hairt wis sair for her an He said, Dinna greet.' He saw
wee things. 'Luikin up, He saw the weel-aff fowk drappin their
offerins intil the kists o the Temple Treasurie an forbye them He
saw a needfu widda drap in a couple o farthins, an He said "Atweill.
I tell ye, this peer woman his pitten in mair nor tham aa."' He saw
throwe things. 'Jesus noo left the Temple, an, as He gaed alang, the
disciples cam up an bade Him look up at the Temple biggins. "Ye
see aa that?" he said, "Atweill, I tell ye, there's nae a steen there that
wull be left abeen anither: the hale Temple will be left a rickle."'

If there's een o the Gospel writers that stauns oot abeen the lave
for giein us a picter o the Jesus that observes fowk, it's St Luke.
Luke shows us the observant Jesus. Nae muckle slips His notice. For
example: Zacchaeus. Zacchaeus speels up a tree in order tae catch
a glisk o the Lord, because naebody likes Zacchaeus eneuch tae lat
him win near tae the front o the crowd: a desperate ploy, tae mak
on you're a loon again, climmin a tree! An faat daes the Lord dee?
– 'When Jesus cam tae the bit, he luikit up an said til him – "Heast
ye, sclim doon, Zacchaeus!"' – an dinna tell me there wisna some
girnin, an pechin, an some sayin: 'Lord, dinna bother wi him, he's
juist a heid bummer in the tax yon!'

In the verra same chapter, the Lord draas near tae Jerusalem.
'Faan He saw the toon He began tae greet,' says Luke. Faat brocht
the tears? He *saw* the toon. He saw faat wis hidden ahin its braw
façade.

Or, the last example, bit there's dizzens mair – Luke tells us that
Jesus wis socht for His denner wi een o the Pharisees. They're aa
sittin doon faan a woman comes in an weeps at His feet, an dries up
her tears wi the hair on her heid. The Pharisee, black-affrontit, maks
on tull himsel that she's nae there. Bit the Lord disna lat him aff wi
it. 'Simon,' he says, 'dae ye see this woman?' Dae ye *see* this woman?

Lord, teach us tae see You
In aa the places
We dinna expect Ye,
Startin wi the roch cradle
In Bethlehem aa the wye
Tae the roch timmer

O the tree faar they lifted Ye
At Calvary because
You hid become the Zacchaeus
Naebody likit eneuch.

Teach us tae see You
Faar You tell't us
You wid be.
In the hungert,
The thirsty,
The ootlin,
The nakit,
The sick,
In the jile.
In aa the fowk we mak invisible
Because we dinna wint
Tae see them.

In aa the fowk we value least
Because we think
They dinna coont.

Lord, teach us tae see You
On ilka road,
Especially the lang road
Tae Emmaus.
Traivel aside's
Faan oor herts are sair,
An though oor een be steikit
Help us tae ken
Foo near at haun You are.

The best o't is that Jesus taks the bairn intil His airms, an it's that – it's that aleen – that tells the twal disciples faat he wints them aa tae ken. He wints them aa tae ken foo weel he understauns that inside ilka een o them there is a hurtin sowl, a sense o emptiness, a longin for attention, that only God his love eneuch tae touch an lift an soothe awa. Faan He pits His airm roon the little een, He's pittin

His airm roon the bairn that bides inside His little band o fishermen an taxmen and ploomen that He's made His friens ...

the disappinted bairn
                        in Judas Iscariot?
the waesome bairn
                        in Simon o Canaan?
the spiled bairn
                        in Thaddaeus?
the feart bairn
                        in Jeames, Alphaeus' laddie?
the timorous bairn
                        in Tammas?
the toustie bairn
                        in Matthew?
the sprosie bairn
                        in Bartholomew?
the mislaired bain
                        in Philip?
the carnaptious bairn
                        in Andra?
the jailous bairn
                        in John?
the hame-drauchtit bairn
                        in Jeames his brither?
the bairn bowdent wi pride
                        in Simon Peter?

The bairn in me an the bairn in you that sulks, fyles, aboot foo roch the world is, foo coorse we're treated, foo fowk tak us for granted, foo we're nivver loved eneuch ... the bairn inside us that longs tae be a somebody.

Jesus says: you are a somebody. Look. Use yer een. This is foo weel, foo wullinly, God loves you. He pits His airms roon ye, like I dae with this wee laddie, or maybe it's a lassie, an He hauds ye ticht.

We dinna ken the bairn's name, dae we? But we dinna hae tull. For the bairn is aa o's.

God the First
an Hinmaist,
Beginnin an end,
we trust You tae haud us
in this life
an the life tae come.
You nivver lat us go.

Christ the Lord,
we trust You
noo an at aa times
tae haud us
throwe the desert
an aa temptations;
throwe the storm
an ilka bluffart;
climmin the stey brae
an ilka challenge;
in ony Gethsemane
faar we feel maist aleen;
on ony cross o pain
we're made tae cairry;
throwe daith itsel
faan neither mirk nor shadda
steik oor een
tae keep us fae kennin
foo near at haun Ye are.

Jesus is imagined following the disciples on a journey, the disciples ahead. They start quarrelling about who is the greatest, and Jesus uses a child to teach them. Here it is thought the child might have been with the group all the time, but noticed only by Jesus. The scene is used to illustrate how divisive the Church is when it gets ahead of Jesus. The child is used also to illustrate the childish attitudes of disciples then and now.

A Scots Communion Prayer

O faither o mercie an God o consolin,
seein aa that draas breath caa you maister
an Lord, it faas tae us richtly an truly,
made as we are by the wark o your hauns,
tae revere you an heeze up the glorie
that hansels your name: without devaul.
First, for the reason that ye hae created us
like tae yersel, but maist o aa ye hae rypit
the jaas o death an damnation an set us free,
the bondage o Satan broken, a thing nae man
nor angel wis able tae dee.
You, Lord, rich in mercie an replete wie guidness,
redeemed us for sure an forever in him
we caa son of the highest, the anely son
an the weel-looed son as weel.
You gave him tae us in the form o man,
sib tae us aa barrin sin itsel,
that in flesh an bleid he micht thole
the sairest pain for aa we did wrang,
his deein the mark o your justice,
his risin the end o the author o death.
He brocht life an hope tae the warld,
an the bairns o Adam cam hame.
Lord, we ken weel that naebody hauds in their heid
the length, the breadth, the depth
an the hicht o the love supreme
you showed us ayont aa the dool
we truly deserved.

You gaed us a promise an you gaed us life
ower aa the domain o death, wha thocht he
had won. You invited us back tae coorie intae
the airms o grace, though there we could still be
thrawn an fecht against you.

O Lord, blin ees that tak their authority fae aa that we get wrang
will nivver gie you the richtsome praise for aa ye hae gien us: yet,
aa the same, harkin tae faat he tellt us, we present oorsels at this his
table, the table he his left us tae mind on him till he comes again, tae
mak braid an clear tae aa the warld that by him aleen we hae gotten
us libertie an life: tae be siccar that by him aleen you ain us bairns
an heirs: by him aleen we hiv access tae the throne o grace: by him
aleen we are safe an secure in oor spiritual kingdom, tae feast an
drink at his table.

Wi him we shall presently share the conversation o heaven ... an
he will tak us up fae the yird an gie us that joy that canna be ended,
the joy you hae readied, Faither o mercie, for aa them you socht an
claimed, lang syne, afore the foons o the earth wis sattled.

An aa these maist winnerfu gledsome delichts we ascribe tae you,
aa fae your mercie, aa fae your grace, throwe the ane an only son
Jesus the Christ: for him this gaitherin o fowk set alicht by the Holy
Spirit, render you thanks an prayer an glorie, for aye an for aye.

*This prayer offers thanks for our creation and redemption and the
death and resurrection of Jesus, who invites people to his table now
and offers us the unending joy of heaven.*

A Scots Communion Service (1)

Minister: The Lord be wi ye.
Response: An wi you tae.
M: Faa kens us like God kens us?
R: Ilk een bar neen, baith young an aul.
M: Baith great an smaa. He kens the gweed things
R: We wid like tae dae bit dinna.
M: He kens the wrang things we canna help deein.
R: Bit gin we come tae Him
M: Doon-hairtit, disjaskit
R: He winna leave us waesome
M: He wull mak aathing richt,
R: Spleet new and braw again.

M: O Jesus, Breid of life, it shud be mett and drink tull's
              tae dee faat
              You said an tae luve een anither, bit we hae luved
              wirsels.
              Jesus, Licht o the warld, we tine Your flame an syne
              the mirk bumbases us.
              Jesus, Yett o the bucht, we gyang wir ain wyes an
              stravaig awa fae You.

R: Christ, hae mercie,
M: Lord, hae mercie.

Aathegither: The Lord hae mercie on's an pit awa wir sins. The
              Lord gie us stieve hairts an wullin hauns tae wark the
              wark o Him that brocht us intae the Kingdom o His
              licht an luve. Sae lat it be.

M: On the nicht He wis haaled i the nets o hate the Lord took breid, blissed it, an broke it. He said 'This is My bodie, gien for you. Dae this tae mind on Me.' An He took the tassie and He said 'This is My bleed, skailed for you. Dae this tae mind on me.'

M: Lift up yer hairts.
R: We lift them up until the Lord
M: Lat's aa gie thanks tae God.
R: Richt an gweed it is.
M: Richt and gweed aagate an athoot devaul. Holy Lord, Faither o aa micht, God Ivverlaistin, it faa's tull's tae gie You thanks an praise an cry You glorious, Maister and Makar o aa things, King o Heiven. Noo may the kirk abeen in glorie an the kirk on the yird tak up the timeless sang wi a single vyce:

Holy, holy, holy Lord God o Hosts,
Heiven an earth are foo o your glorie:
Glorie be tae you, Lord abeen.
Blissit is he that comes i the name o the Lord!
Hosanna in the hichts!

M: Sae noo we mind on Him, as He his bidden. He wis born for's in a steadin an beddit faar the kye waur.
R: Glorie tae You, the bairn o Mary.
M: He wis baptized i the Jordan watters for's, tested i the desert, an He sent the Deil hame tae think again.
R: Glorie tae You, Christ o the desert.
M: He made the lamiter walk, He raised up the deid. Luve wis the sang He threapit tull His ain fowk an fremmit fowk alike.
R: Glorie tae You, Christ o healin.
M: He was bocht an sell't for siller, gien ower tae Pilate, condemned tae the cross; for us He tholed it aa, for us He dee'd.
R: Glorie tae You, Christ o the timmer.
M: For us He rose again wie the soothfast wird that He wull aye be wi His leal friens, aye, e'en tae the en o the ages.
R: Glorie tae You, Christ o risin.

M: He gaed tae the Faither.

R: Eident Intercessor, we wyte for You, for the day naebody kens, nor yet the oor, save You an the Faither, faan You wull come again.

Great is the mystery o faith:
Christ his dee'd,
Christ is risen,
Christ wull come again.

M: Tull that day comes, we dee this.
   We tak breid an wine.
   We mind faat He said:
   This is my bodie
   This is my bleed
   Bliss, Lord, this breid wi the pooer o the Halie Speerit.
   Bliss, Lord, this wine wi the pooer o the Halie Speerit.
   Lat them be tull us the Communion o His bodie and bleed.
   Lamb o God that taks awa the sin o the warld,

R: Grant us Your peace.
   The breid is broken for the life o the warld.

PRAYER EFTER COMMUNION

M: The Shalom o God be wi ye.
   Lat us pray.
   Faither o us aa,
   We bliss Yer Name
   For the breid o life eternal,
   For the royal wine o heiven.

   We thank Ye for bringin us tae this boord
   Faar there is neither aul nor young,
   Walthy nor peer,
   Frien nor ootlin,
   Bleck nor fite,
   Wumman nor man,
   Bit ae femmly.

We thank Ye that here the warld ayont
An the warld we bide in
Are jined an faistened thegither.
Noo, so that faat we share
Shudna neither be selfish nor nerra,
For the peace o the yird we pray,
For an en tae wars an famines an drouths;
For aa them that want hoose or hame;
For them that mourn;
For them that are tholin pain o bodie,
Pain o mind or speerit.

Lord, in Yer mercie hear us
For oor ain fowk, near or far.
Hear us for aa this pairish roon aboot,
For aa the kirks faar yer Name is glorifiet.

Bliss this oor native laan,
As the bairns o Scotlan here an faarivver.
For Jesus' sake, sae lat it be.

This prayer of consecration follows in Scots the traditional pattern and the familiar words of the Church of Scotland Communion service; and the post-Communion prayer gives thanks for the inclusiveness of faith and prays for peace for the world and help for the needy.

A Scots Communion Service (2)

Christ, oor Passowre Lamb, hes been saicrificed: and ee behuive tae keep oor Passowre, no wi the auld barm, the barm o vice an wickitness, but wi the barmless breid o aefauldness an truith.

God maist high, You read oor herts like open beuks: You ken oor craves: cleanse the thochts o oor herts wi the inspiration o Your Holy Spirit, so's we can love You the richt gate an gie Your name oor leal an ample praise.

Father in Heiven, we confess that we hae broken Your commaunds an gaen oor ain wyes; deen things tae please oorsels an nivver mine the lave; we had been prood and thrawn; we hae cairried the name o Christ an yet we've cairried on as gin we nivver kent Him –

    Lord hae mercie on us.
(R) Christ hae mercie on us.
    Lord hae mercie on us.

God forgie us; God in His mercie help us noo tae come tae the Holy Table wi open herts, throwe Jesus Christ oor Lord.

    The Lord be wi ye.
(R) An wi yersel.
    Lift up yer herts.
(R) We lift 'em up until the Lord.
    Let's aa gie thanks tae God.
(R) It is richt and gweed.

It is. At aa times an in ilka place it faa's tills tae gie thanks tae you.

Holy Lord, Father o aa micht, ivverlaistin God, we cry You glorious, maister an makar o aa things; You, King o' Heiven, we praise
an worship.

Wi aa the thrang o Heiven's fowk, wi the Kirk abeen in glory, we
praise an worship You –

Holy, holy, holy, Lord God o Hosts.
Heiven an earth are foo o Your glorie.
Glorie be tae You, O Lord Maist Heich.

Blissed is the Een that comes i the Lord's Name!
Hosanna far abeen an aawye!

Sae noo, we bring tae mind oor Saviour Christ – the wecht o wae He
shoodered for's on Calvary, His risin fae the dwam o daith tae tak
His place aside the Faither faar He spiks for's, eident Intercessor. An
we tak tent o this, that we bide wytin for the day faan He will come
again till's.

Sen doon, O Lord, Your Holy Spirit upon his an on Your breid an
wine, set here afore You, that this breid micht be for aa o's a sharin
o the body o Christ, an this cup a sharin o the bleed o Christ; so that
we micht tak them in faith an sae be friens een till the ither an friens
tae Him the heid o ilka boord.

An here we offer You, God an Faither, oor sauls an bodies for
You tae use an bliss. An this oor praise an thanks we offer tee: in
mercie reck it oor weel-farrant wark.

The grace o the Lord Jesus Christ be wi ye aa.

'Faat I tauld ye cam doon tae me frae the Lord, an it is this – the Lord
Jesus, on the nicht whan he wis betrayed, tuik a laif an, efter he hed
speired the blissin, brak it an said: "This is my bodie at is gien for ye:
dae this in remembrance o me." I the same wey, whan the sipper wis
by, he tuik the caup an said: "This caup is the new Covenant, sealed
wi my bleed: dae this, as aften as ye drink it, in remembrance o me.
For ilka time at ye ait this breid an drink this caup, ye proclaim the
Lord's daith, till he comes."'

Lamb o God, that taks awa the sins o the warld –
(R) Hae mercie on us.
Lamb o God, that taks awa the sins o the warld –
(R) Hae mercie on us.
Lamb o God, that taks awa the sins o the warld –
(R) Grant us Your peace.

* * *

The Peace o the Lord Jesus Christ be wi ye aa.

Faither o's aa, we thank an praise You, for that we, faan we wis hyne awa, hae been brocht near: eence we wis ootlins but noo we're burgess toonsmen o the saints, God's femmly an nae mistak, sib tae the Christ Your ae an ane Son. Aa throwe His life an in the mainner o His daith He brocht Your love till's, He gaed us grace, He caa'd ajee the yett o glorie. We that hae pairt an lot wi Him wid fain, wi Him, pree Resurrection life; we that slocken the saul's drouth here wid fain bring aaitherbody life; we that the Spirit lowses fae the mirk wid fain caa licht abreed for een an aa tae traivel by.

An may oor Lord Jesus Christ himsel an God oor Father, at hes luved us an gien us lestin comfort an guid howp throwe His grace, comfort oor hairts an mak us stainch in aathing guid, be it wark or wurd!

Amen.

The Lord o Peace Himsel gie us peace aagate an wioot devaul. The Lord be wi ye aa.

HOLY COMMUNION

Oot o the bleeze o summer suns an dowie rain
oot o the hairst, the breid
(lift up the bread)

oot o the vine, its sweetness an purple
oot o the brae-face, heavy wi fruit: the wine
(lift up the wine)

49

the saft days o summer come tae the Table
an the sair nicht He kent the betrayal, His friens roon aboot Him,
gethered like us tae be siccar in mindin Him.

We dae weel tae be here.
The Lord be wi ye.
We dae weel tae be here.
Lift up yer herts.
We dae weel tae be here.
Lat's gie the Lord thanks.
It is richt we should: we can dae nae ither: for He his been
mornin licht fan the dark wid hae smored us,
an He his been welcome nicht fan the day wis ower lang.
He his been breid fan we wis in want,
a frien on the road fan the road wis teem,
an His stave wis stoot an swack tae defend
fan the glen wis happit in mirk an shaddas.
He his been true till Himsel
an nivver left us aleen tae greet
though sair wis the wae we warsled wi.
For aa that, an aa that, we praise the Name
abeen ilkae name, the Name o the one King an Lord
traivellin the laich road o the human wye
tae bring us wi mercy hame
tae the buchts o grace, the bield o delicht:
the ring on wir finger, the robe on oor shooders
the feast an the ceilidh.

This is the feast o them that come hame, prodigal sons
an prodigal dothers. We dae weel tae be here.
So we lift the sang, or we say it thegither,
the sang o the angels,
the sang o them that are risen ...
Holy, holy, holy, Lord God o hosts
Heiven an earth are foo o your glory
Glory tae you, o Lord abeen aa.
Blessed is he that comes i the name o the Lord,
Hosanna i the hichts.

Blessed the Bairn that wis born o Mary,
blessed the Man, the Lamb, i the Jordan,
blessed the Teacher, thrang i the streets,
blessed the Healer, blessed the Fisher o men,
an the Herd o the lost, the Gate o the sheep,
blessed the Redeemer, true till Himsel,
climmin the tree o oor grief
tae bring us the gledness o God:
Risin in mornin licht tae announce His Easter,
an Easter for aa: for He comes till His ain
nae eence, nae twice, nae juist the Bethlehem nicht o stars,
nae juist the gairden weet wi dyowe far He met the weemin,
bit ony an aa times we are thegether, be it twa or three
that are met in His Name:
He is there in the midst.
this is the mystery:
Christ his deed
Christ is risen
Christ will come again
Till that day dawns (we ken nae fan: it could be the morn,
or a thoosan eers)
We dae faat He said: we brak the Breid
An we tak the Cup. We dae weel tae be here.

Bless tae us, Lord, this Breid.
Bless tae us, Lord, this Cup.
Lat them be till us the Communion o the bodie
an bleed o the Christ: lat them be health an haleness
till aa that are here.

Sae lat it be.

Here, bread and wine represent soft summer days and the sad night
of betrayal, and so the light after darkness and a welcome at the end
of the day. This is a feast for prodigals who have returned.

The 23rd Psalm o King Dauvit (1)

My herd is the Lord, sae wants I hae neen,
I lie doon at ease in howes that are green.
Aside the saft souch o burns rinnin clean
He leads me at peace noo an aye.

My saul he restores again an again,
Wyes better tae tak he shows me tae ain,
For the sake o the richt an glorious name
That is his aleen noo an aye.

Though roch be the road an I traivel near
Tae mirk an meshanter, nocht wull I fear.
Close tee tae haun aye, your stave is my fier,
My gledness an howp noo an aye.

Faes tae the left of me, faes tae the richt
I feast like a king, by day or by nicht.
Anointed an blythe an full'd wi delicht
I nivver ging boss noo an aye.

Lang as my days are, I trus in the pooer
O mercy tae haud me safe an secure
For I hae a bield faar walcome is sure,
The hoose o the Lord noo an aye.

*A Scots version of the familiar metrical form of the 23rd psalm. The
'herd' suggests more than a shepherd but one who watches over the
sheep in an unfenced and therefore dangerous area.*

The 23rd Psalm o King Dauvit (2)

The Lord's ma herd, A'll want for nocht,
He gars me ti ly doun
In gressie howes, an syne A'm brocht
Far wimplin burnies croun.

An far for ither joys A craik
An wanner faur frae God,
He airts me, for His ain name's sake,
Intil His ain richt road.

Ay, tho A gang throu yon derk glen
Far waesum shadaes faw
He'll keep near-haun me, an A ken
A'll hae nae fear ava.

Tho monie foes around me staun
His kyndness niver fails;
He spreids ma table, an His haun
Fills ma cup til it skails.

Een sae, gweed gydin an gweed-gree
Gang wi me ilka day;
An in God's houss far up on hie
A fain wad byde for aye.

The Apache Blissin

A Scots translation of the Apache Blessing

Fae noo on in ye winna feel
Nae rain
For ye will be a bield een tae
The ither.
Fae noo on in ye winna feel
Nae caul
For ye will hap een anither
Snod eneuch.
Fae noo on in ye are twa fowk
Wi bit a single life aheid o ye.
G'waa noo tae yer ain hame
An the days ye'll share
Egither.
May thet be lang and gween.
Mind an think weel o yersels
An o een anither
An bring tae mind time an
Again
Fit brocht ye thegither in the
First place.
Ye baith deserve the best that
Ye can offer
Een anither the best o
Kindness
Sweetened
Aye wi tenner herts. Try an
Nae faa aneth
The best.

Roch times may come – they
Come tae aabody – but
Nivver tine yer haud o the
Things ye are maist sure o.
They coont for far mair than
The odd meshanter.
Fit ye hae richt an siccar will
Help ye warsle throwe
Aa the coorse days fin the
Cloods are laich ... Nivver
Forget that the sun is still
There even though we
Canna aye see it.
An gin ye baith tak an equal
Haud o the ploo-shafts
Tae raise up a bonny fur, yer
Hairst will be aa the gowd an
Plenty ye could wish for.
May joy be wi ye.

This is a form of blessing to be used at a marriage, and wishes the couple the best of kindness for each other but asks them to hold on to what matters about each other if times are difficult.

Twal Scottish Icons

A litany

VRICHT
Makar o aa things,
Christ the vricht.
SMITH
Sorter o connached things,
Christ the smith.
FISHER
Redder o roch seas,
Christ the fisher.
HERD
Eident kenner,
Christ the herd.
PLOOMAN
Brakker o falla grun,
Christ the plooman.
TOON-KEEPER
Gaird o the forhooiet,
Christ the toon-keeper.
GRIEVE
Rowster o sweir chiels,
Christ the grieve.
ORRAMAN
Maister o aa trades,
Christ the orraman.
BAXTER
Banisher o aa want,
Christ the baxter.

MINER
Howker o braw seams,
Christ the miner.
DYKER
Bigger wi bare haunds,
Christ the dyker.
PIPER
Stirrer o hert's bluid,
Christ the piper.

connached – spoiled; redder – settler; eident – diligent; kenner –
overseer; gaird – guard; forhooiet – forsaken; rowster – stirrer; sweir
– reluctant; orraman – odd-job man; baxter – baker; bigger – builder.

This litany compares Jesus to the the traditional names for workers
associated with farming.

Canticle o the Lamb

A Scots translation of Revelation 5:12

Worthie is the Lamb
That wis slain
Tae hae gien untae Him
Pooer an wyss-ness, honour an glorie,
Blissin fae ilka airt.

Worthie are You, Jesus,
Lamb o God

Faa taks awa the sin o the warld,
Lamb o God nae blaudit wi ony blaud.

This is a Scots translation of Revelation 5:12 about the sinless Lamb of God who takes away the sin of the world.

A Litany o the Days o the Redeemer

Incidents in the life of Jesus

Christ o Mary
Christ o the nowt's troch
Christ o the temple
Christ o the watters o Jordan
Christ o the wird
Christ o the bare meers
Christ o the lochside
Christ o the waddin in Cana
Christ o the heich corries
Christ o the sainin
Christ o the lanely prayer
Christ o the five rowies, the twa mackerel
Chirst o the shalt
Christ o the whang o lowss tows
Christ o the double-heidit maik
Christ o the bruckle breid
Christ o the tassie
Christ o the gairden caa'd Gethsemane
Christ o the sleekit kiss
Christ o the chines
Christ o the palace yaird
Christ o the plainstanes
Christ o the powky jags
Christ o the stey brae
Christ o the rippit sark
Christ o the nails
Christ o the promises
Christ o the wersh wine

Christ o the last drooth
Christ o the rippit veil
Christ o the fell mirk
Christ o the lood seeven
Christ o silence
Christ o the steikit side
Christ o the mort-claith
Christ o wytin
Christ o risin
Christ o surprises
Christ o the barred chaumer
Christ o the teem nets
Christ o the stappit nets
Christ o the greeshoch
Christ at the Faither's side
Strident intercessor
Christ o oor nichts
Christ o oor days
Hae mercie on us.

nowts – cattle; meers – moors; sainin – blessing; shalt – donkey; whang – whipping; tows – ropes; bruckle – broken; chines – cheeks; plainstanes – courtyard; powky – prickly; stey – steep; fell mirk – terrible darkness; wytin – reproaches; chaumer – chamber; greeshoch – glowing fire.

This litany describes the life of Jesus through using incidents or moments in the life of Jesus, or features such as the burial cloth or the bursting nets.

A Walin fae the Sangs o Dauvit

A Scots translation of Psalm 139:7–12

Foo far, O God, foo far
Div I hae tae gyang
Afore I'm ayont Your seein een?
Is there nae wye ataa tae jouk Ye?

I cud climm the hichts
Bit ye're there aheid o me.
Gin I took the laich road tae the laan o the mirk
Ye wid be there aareadies.

Gin I cud tak tae the lift an flee
Like a bird at the crack o day,
Gin I put oceans ahin me, there anaa
Ye wid keep me an gaird me,
Yer richt haun stieve an ticht aroon me.

Gin I said 'Hide me fae even the face o the meen,
Hap me in smorin nicht'
Tae You the dour dark his naething tae say,
The nicht cudna bleck me: for wi You
The hairt o the dark his a lowe
Bricht as a simmer sin.

How far do I have to go before I am beyond your seeing eye?

Christ afore us, Christ ahint us

Christ before us, Christ behind us

Saviour an Lord,
You gyang afore us,
You traivel in front o's.
You map the grun we dinna
    ken,
An there's naewye we gyang
But You hinna been there.

Saviour and Lord,
You go before us,
You travel in front of us.
You map the ground we don't
    know,
And there's nowhere we go
But you have not been there.

Christ o the desert: there is
Nae temptation You hinna
Faced an focht for's.

Christ of the desert: there is
No temptation you have not
Faced and fought for us.

Christ o the storm on the face
O the loch: there is
Nae chaos You canna quaeten.

Christ of the storm on the surface
Of the loch: there is
No chaos you cannot still.

Christ o the brae-face: there is
Nae hunger You canna meet.

Christ of the hillside: there is
No hunger you cannot meet.

Christ o the gairden o
    Gethsemane:
There is nae loneliness
You hinna tholed.
Christ o the stobs: there is
Nae insult You hinna carried.

Christ of the Garden of
    Gethsemane:
There is no loneliness
You have not endured.
Christ of the thorns: there is
No insult you have not carried.

Christ o the nails: there is Nae weird You hinna dree'd.	Christ of the nails: there is No fate you have not dreaded.
Christ o risin: You gyang In front o's tae prepare a place For's, so that faar You are, We micht be anaa.	Christ of rising, You go In front of us to prepare a place For us, so that where you are, We may be also.
Gin we gyang up tae heiven, You are there.	If we go up to heaven, You are there.
Gin we mak oor bed in daith, Again we find Ye.	If we rest in death, Again we find you.

So: richtly, gledly, blithely,
We proclaim You,
Risen Lord
Christ afore us.
But here: here, Lord, on the
  wye
Tae Capernaum,
I jaloose Ye were ahint
The Twal.
I hear Ye tell em,
Caa forrit, lads,
Gie me some space.
I hear them, contermashious
  chiels,
Come back, at Ye –
Bide wi's, Jesus,
We're weariet athoot Ye.
Bit Ye wid hae neen o't –
Caa forrit, lads, Ye said.
	So: rightly, gladly, cheerfully,
	We proclaim you,
	Risen Lord
	Christ ahead of us.
	But here: here, Lord, on the
	  way
	To Capernaum,
	I realise you were behind
	The Twelve.
	I hear you tell them,
	Go ahead, lads,
	Give me some space.
	I hear them, argumentative
	  men,
	Reply to you –
	Stay with us, Jesus,
	We're exhausted without you.
	But you would have none of it –
	Come forward, lads, you said.

An sae they did. They traivelled athoot Him. An they fell tae fechtin.	And so they did. They travelled without him. And they started fighting.

Saviour an Lord,
Is there nae here
A parable for aa Your kirks,
That we traivel athoot Ye
At oor peril?
That near twa thoosan eer
Efter Ye were happit
In a spare troch in Bethlehem
We're still fechtin
Aboot faa's the greatest?

Saviour an Lord,
Traivel ahin's
As lang as Ye maun:
But we need You tae
Tae bring us tae book
An tae say tull's fyles:
Faat are Ye fechtin aboot?

Traivel ahin's,
Catch faat we miss,
Catch faa we miss,
Faan the fishers o men
Get tied up in knots
An forget their nets.

Saviour and Lord,
Is there not here
A parable for all your churches,
That we travel without you
At our peril?
That nearly two thousand years
After you were swaddled
In a bare stable in Bethlehem
We are still fighting
About who is the greatest?

Saviour and Lord,
Travel behind us,
As long as you must:
But we need you also
To bring us to book,
And to say to us sometimes:
What are you fighting about?

Travel behind us,
Catch what we miss,
Catch whom we miss,
When the fishers of men
Get tied up in knots
And forget their nets.

The Lord's Prayer in Scots

Faither o's aa, bidin abeen, Your name be halie; lat Your reign
gang forrit, an Your will be daen here, as it's daen abeen. Gie us
oor breid this day. Forgie the wrangs we've vrocht, as we forgie
the wrangs we dree. Lat nae temptation pit's agley, bit keep us
weel roadit. For the Kingdom is Yours, Yours the Micht an the
Glorie, forivver an aye. Sae lat it be.

Auld Hunnert

The 100th Psalm o King Dauvit

Aw ye fowk at dis bide on yird
Lilt til the Lord wi cantie vyce.
Him sair fou blythe; His praise mak heard.
Cum ye afore Him an rejyce.

Ken at the Lord is God an see
Wioot wir aid He did us mak.
We are his fowk; wir herd is He,
An for His hirsel dis us tak.

Lauch at thae yetts as ye gae ben
Cum til His courts wi speirits licht.
Bliss honour magnifee an ken,
At it is wycelik braw an richt.

Ay, for the Lord wir God is guid.
His maircies is for ivver shair.
His sickaries frae lang syne stuid,
An bydes for ayte an ivvermair.

Ti Faither Son and Speirit ane,
The God at Heiven an yird wad sair,
Be glorie as in ages gaen,
As nou an as fir ivvermair.

Amen

Robbing the Dark

A poem from the stable to empty tomb

By a new star wonder finds us,
Comes a light that heals and blinds us.
Comes the one the ages prayed for,
Comes the one all things were made for.
By a new star and a new way
Comes the one who is the true way:
King of heaven, born of woman,
Hope and promise crown his coming.

In the desert, evil tries him,
Fame and glamour tantalize him;
But with power he resists them,
Love his song and love his system.
Pride and pomp he leaves behind him,
Glad to let the glory find him
True at last and true forever
To the bonds he cannot sever.

In the city, silver buys him,
Friend and foe alike despise him;
Man of sorrows left to die,
Raised up on the cross so high
Till the day of glad surprises,
Robs the dark of death's disguises,
And with eyes made clear they see him,
Risen king who comes to free them.

From Lent to Easter

A meditation

Easter pulls us forward, during the days of Lent, with a magnetic power all of its own. In fact, if we keep Lent at all seriously, the more we enter the wilderness of soul-searching and sombre poverty before God, the more we need the riches of Easter Day. As the Orthodox Church has it, Easter is the Chosen and Holy Day, the one King and Lord of Sabbaths ... the Feast of Feasts.

I once experienced the Russian Orthodox Easter Service in London. About 11pm, people began to assemble in the cathedral in Ennismore Gardens, some standing in groups, some chatting, some lighting candles in front of icons, some going forward to kiss the shroud which symbolizes Christ buried in the tomb.

Very rapidly the church filled up, all age groups mingling, most of us standing, expectantly, as the clock moved towards midnight. Old ladies in black shawls and black scarves flitted about, or sought some of the few seats which are made available for this marathon act of worship. We were soon launched into the unforgettable Easter Vigil. Metropolitans and priests took it in turn to give the time-honoured announcement – *Christos Voskrose Christos Avesti*. Christ is Risen! And each time, the packed cathedral resounded and ecstatic response – he is risen indeed!

The following poem is a far cry from the multi-lingual, traditional Russian celebration. It is an attempt, though, to find another language for the story of Jesus' life, death and rising again. Not another language, really, but another medium. So, cue drums and synthesizer, lay down a fast beat, and let's go for it: the 'Resurrection Rap'!

He was a preacher and a teacher. He turned water into wine
He said 'I am the Light and the Light will shine'
He cured the lame and the sightless eyes
He said 'I am the bread and the bread will rise'
He told of a kingdom and a kingdom's dawn
He said 'I am the Way and the Way goes on'
He walked on the water and he hushed the sea
He said 'I am the Truth, I will make you free'
He fed the crowd on the mountain-side
He said 'Bring me your poor and your terrified'
He consoled the sad and he dried their tears
He said 'Give me your pain. Give me your fears'
He told a story 'bout a Prodigal Son
He said 'Bring me your drop-outs, whatever they've done'
He crossed all borders and he broke all rules
He said 'Give me your losers. Give me your fools'
He died the death of an innocent man
But he dreamed His dreams and he followed His plan
His name was Jesus, he came to the town
When the die was cast and the chips were down
And His enemies waited for a chance to strike
At a man whose dream they did not like
He taught in the Temple, He taught in the street
He arranged a meal for His friends to eat
He said 'Sharing love is the way to be
This is my body: Remember me'
There were twelve true men but I'm sad to say
That one was tricked for a traitor's pay
There were twelve in all – you know their names
Matthew, Thomas, Andrew, James
Simon, John, Bartholomew
Thaddaeus, Simon, James number two
A man called Philip, and a man to blame,
And Judas Iscariot was his name
He made a bargain and he drew a map
To help the soldiers lay a deadly trap
And they captured Jesus at dead of night

And they marched Him off without a fight
A prisoner who had done no wrong
But sing for us all His freedom song
'I am the life and you live in me
I am the Truth; I will make you free'
'What's the truth?' said Pilate 'Take Him away
Let the crowd decide and have their say'
And the crowd roared out with furious cries
'The thief goes free and Jesus dies'
They flogged Him then with mockery
And they led Him away to Calvary
Step by step he climbed that street
To hang in the glare of the noonday heat
A robber to the left, a robber to the right
The sky above grew back as night
Till it was over at the stroke of three
The prisoner died and His soul was free
The man was finished or so they said
But they got it wrong when they thought Him dead
For the plan was greater than a cross of wood
The dream wasn't dead, and the news is good
They thought it was over, they said 'Goodbye'
And they borrowed a grave for the man to lie
The morning came, and the evening too
The dawn next day was a brilliant blue
When the women came at break of day
To the place they thought His body lay
They came to find Him and they found Him gone
The cage was empty and the bird had flown!
The grave was empty, for the plan was clear
'The Lord has risen! He is not here!'
And they ran with dancing feet to share
The amazing news that the tomb was bare
'The Lord is risen! Lift up your hearts!
This is where the beginning starts!'

Looking for the Blueprint

A prayer for the first Sunday of Lent

Christ, who was tested in the desert, glory to You.
You resisted the invasion of Your secret self.
You refused to listen to Your vanity.
Your sense of purpose did not waver.
You held back from the dreaming of unfaithful dreams.
Glory to You.
What was it that alerted You, Son of Man, to the hollow voices?
Was it the great ones who had lived *before* You? Lonely prophets
and poets of Israel who had themselves been refined and purified in
the fires of testing? Did their victories speak to You, did their songs
ring in Your ears? Did You remember them and lift up Your heart?
What was it alerted You, Son of Man, in the desert's emptiness?
Was it the thought of those who would come *after* You?
The ones who would lack Your resolve, Your self-possession,
Your clarity of vision, Your hold of God, God's hold of You?
People driven to desperate measures, people racked with doubt,
People compromised by their indecision and paralyzed by fear?
People like us?
Did You hear us, maybe, before we had spoken, beg You for a
leadership only You could give, a landmark only you could build?
Lord, we are still begging.
Still looking for the blueprint.

Lord, have mercy upon us.
May God in His goodness turn our desert places
      into gateways to new life,
            opportunities for new obedience.

And may he turn us again to Himself,
                    cleaned and refreshed,
Through Jesus Christ our Lord.
AMEN.

The Journey

A prayer for Lent

Let the praises of God
resound in this place
to the one who is timeless
from us who are caught
between yesterday and tomorrow:
To the one who is and will be
from us who are caught
between the darkness and the light.

Meet with us here, Redeemer Lord,
that we may offer you
praise on the Lenten journey.
Guide us to where your pain
is given for all, for our pardon and peace.
Wounded one, king of the sorrows,
Grant us your healing and wholeness.
Conqueror of death, bring us
to that majestic morning
when the tomb was seen to be bare,
your shroud but an empty shell,
your stone rolled away.

Spirit of flame that kindles hope,
Spirit of fierce renewal,
lead us in gladness and glee
with a dancing step
into the kingdom's promise.

Caught as we are between a time
to mourn and a time to dance,
let the song begin:
let the trumpets of the resurrection

drown the still sad music
of our failures and defeats,
till all at the last shall be harvest
and your good purposes fulfilled.

Forty Days and Forty Nights

A meditation on Christ in the wilderness

On 7 February 2005, Ellen MacArthur completed her epic, single-handed voyage round the world. Of course she was backed up on shore by her team, but hers was nevertheless a marathon where she was the only one on the boat, alone against the waves and the wind. What massive resources did she have to draw on to pull her through? Let us count the ways she survived and triumphed. Adrenaline? The thrill of the chase? Self-belief? Determination? The refusal to fail? Loyalty? Loyalty to those who had made it possible for her to attempt this, loyalty to the engineers who had built the boat, loyalty to her band of sponsors? Her parents, watching her helplessly as she battled with challenges they had never faced? She had to stay true to their belief in her, and to their willingness to let a loved and cherished daughter put them through anguish, all for the sake of her following her dream. How many times, I wonder, did they wish that their wee girl had gone into something safe, like holding down a career in teaching or being a land-based social worker or a lawyer?

What massive resources sustained Jesus of Nazareth when he entered the desert to begin his marathon of forty days and forty nights alone, alone with the burning sun and the arid landscape, the rocks and the sand, the constant fear that he would become disorientated by the conditions he was subjected to? How do people deal with solitary confinement? And when the desert is your cell, your dungeon, your place of no escape, how do you deal with that?

Adrenaline? Adrenaline kicks in when you know that something big is happening, and you had better not flunk it. In my student days, I saw people like me wired on adrenaline going into exams, nerves jangling and up for it. Or what was it like to sit your driving test? What is it like to be a policeman sent out on an arrest when you know that this is not the best thing that is going to happen to you this week? Or standing up to make that speech that will be listened to with careful attention; climbing up into a pulpit, when your words may be measured ounce by ounce by those who welcome what you say and those who detest what you say?

Self-belief? Self-belief kicks in when you know that what you are doing is what you do best: what you were born for. All else is mere detail: this is the reason you are on this earth. Alexander Pushkin has a poem in which he says:

> poet, heed them not when they praise you,
> heed them not when they lambast you:
> 'you're king' so dwell alone. Your free path tread
> wherever your free mind your steps may lead.

Determination? Determination kicks in when you remember the stuff you are made of, and you remember too that people are watching you to see if you are true to the name you carry, the reputation you own. I love that moment in *The Lord of the Rings* when Gimli the dwarf hesitates at the mouth of the Dimholt mountain, a place of extreme and infamous danger. Aragorn and Legolas have plunged into the swirling mist that obscures the opening to a place of the doomed, and Gimli groans: 'Oh, a dwarf afraid to go underground? I'd never hear the end of it.' He plunges in behind his two companions.

Refusal to fail? This kicks in when you hear in your inner being the mocking laughter of those who want you to fail. You want to steal that laughter away from them, deny them their sneering sense of having seen you beaten. We hear mockery in the tones of the tempter, as Matthew relates to us: 'If you are the Son of God ...' says the demonic voice, the voice that urges Jesus to doubt himself and to exercise magic. Magic done for effect or for applause was never Jesus' way.

Loyalty? Loyalty has two faces – one turned back to the past, one looking forward. Jesus had lonely prophets and the protesters and the poets of Israel to look back to when he resisted in the desert. Men who had been tried and tested and who had won through.

Their victories resonated in his memory. Their songs rang in his ears. And then there were the ones coming after him, who would need his steadiness of purpose, his resolve, his leadership. He was loyal to the unknown ones who would build on what he was doing.

When Ellen MacArthur sailed into Falmouth in triumph, her vessel was surrounded by dozens of smaller craft, by sailors who could never in a hundred years do what she had done, but sailors nonetheless who crept into the shadow of her achievement for the sheer fun of doing so. In the shelter of her triumph they were paying tribute to a survivor, a winner, a ground-breaker. And what else are we doing this morning, when we read the story of the temptations, but hoisting our little sails in honour of the one who came through unscathed his stormy forty days and forty nights?

Spectators of the Redeemer

A meditation for Passion Sunday

What makes a good photograph?

I have in my mind a photograph of the former President Clinton side by side with Nelson Mandela in Mandela's old cell on Robben Island. Is it a great photograph? As an image, of course, it has untold depth: a black man and a white man in the same cell. 'Listen,' I can hear Nelson Mandela saying, 'If you want to understand me, you have to visit this part of my life.' But whether Mr Clinton stayed long enough to catch a hint of the pain or not, we will never know. Looking at him standing by Mandela's side, I wondered whether this was just a visit to someone else's hell, just another photo opportunity for the journalists, just another picture.

But isn't that all we ever do: zoom into other people's misery, watch, gaze, visit, and then zoom away again? Are we not all just spectators?

When schoolchildren were shot some time ago in Jerusalem, for some people the images shown on television will have evoked more than the feeling of spectators: old horrors will have been awakened as they realized with a sense of grief that they had been there. They knew what that mother must have felt like. But in that atrocity in Jerusalem, there was a twist of cruelty, for we were not prepared for the possibility of children killing other children. That is a new horror. We are made into spectators again: the experiences of Dunblane not copied at all but made even worse, made even more inexplicable. This is not meant to happen. We are not ready for this.

I received a phone-call some time ago from a colleague who has gone to work as an assistant minister in a very large, very prestigious church. The minister he will assist has been struck down by a terminal disease and is dying. My friend told me how he had gone to

78

his minister's bedside last week. He said: 'I couldn't help it. I broke down and wept. And I hated myself, for the man's wife was with me. I'm supposed to help, and I burst into tears.' I said: 'Thank God. Your stiff upper lip is far less important than your heart.'

Today is Passion Sunday. In a word, it is a Sunday when the suffering of the Redeemer banishes all other subjects, dismisses every other topic, claims our full attention. Passion Sunday puts us on the alert: it is urgent that now we concentrate on the Redeemer.

I have this photograph of Him in my mind: He is preparing to come to Jerusalem to visit our pain, the awful pain of those who love Him and the pain of those who don't know what to do with Him. The pain of the lonely Roman governor Pontius Pilate and the pain of the crowd, the pain of the lost disciple, and the pain of the loyal 11, the pain of King Herod – jealous, compromised king – and the pain of the thieves who were condemned alongside Him. But what makes Jesus the Redeemer is that He comes not to watch this pain but to live it. He takes it into Himself and makes it bearable. He becomes the prisoner, and Robben Island is just one of his addresses. He becomes the victim of cruelty and spite. Jonesboro, Arkansas, where five students were murdered and ten injured, is just another of his addresses. He becomes the one who is condemned to die, and the terminal ward is yet another of his addresses.

All I have to say today is this: God does not watch us as a spectator. He enters into the pain of where we are, and He takes it into Himself. He transforms it. But be warned. The transformation is gradual; it is never spectacular. And if President Clinton feels for a split second what it feels like to be a prisoner; if the parents in Jonesboro feel for a split second what it means to be in our hearts and prayers; if a man at a bedside forgets his public role and opts to be just a man, then be sure of this: the Redeemer is drawing men and women into His stupendous secret: there are no spectators, there are only those who are prepared to enter into the pain, and face it, and by so doing make it lose its power to diminish us.

Palm Sunday Man

A reflection at the start of Holy Week

Palm Sunday man, who are you?

You are not the teacher who spoke in parables so that others had to think about their meaning. You are not the healer who performed cures and then told people to go and tell no-one. You are not the solitary man who sometimes went off by yourself to be anonymous. You are not the critic of the Pharisees who scolded them for parading their religion.

Today you let go of the person who did good by stealth. Today you choose not to be anonymous. Today you head up your own parade on a beast of burden. Palm Sunday man, who are you?

You never lose your capacity to surprise us. Just when we had you down as a man who sometimes fled from the crowd and the hysteria of crowds, you come to the city with a crowd cheering you on. Just when we thought that you might be content with the acclaim of the one person healed, the single individual set free and the lonely leper brought out of exile, you invite the city to register that you are coming in. Just when we thought that you had only 12 to teach, you enrol a multitude into your school of ideas.

Palm Sunday man, who are you? You were never a self-publicist. You were never a celebrity as we understand that word today. You were never a smooth-tongued teacher, offering cheap rewards to those who flung in their lot with you. In fact, you horrified many who could not cope with the hardships you promised them. Leave everything behind and follow you? Take up a cross and fall in behind you? Love my enemy? Sell my possessions and give to the poor?

Palm Sunday man, who are you?

You are now, as you always are, the one who lives what he teaches. What you say about yourself you are. You say you are the way, the truth and the life. So, the entry into Jerusalem is an affectionate tribute to John the Baptist and his demand: 'Prepare ye the way of the Lord.'

Someone said to me this week: people may not believe what you say, but they believe what you do. The words of Zechariah are brought to glorious flower here: 'This is our king, humble and mounted on an ass, on a foal, the young of a she-ass.' This is one of those times when it is not enough for Jesus to know the Bible: he *becomes* the Bible.

I am the truth.

Truth comes in by the front door, not by some hidden entrance, afraid to show its face. Truth comes in such a way that all can see him, and some can choose to shout 'Hosanna!' And some can choose to mutter 'humbug'. Truth comes demanding a verdict: are you for me or against me? People have often spoken to me of a decisive moment in their lives, when they realized that time had run out for them, and they had to come down on one side or the other of the great divide: Jesus of Nazareth or somebody else, or nobody else. I think the Jesus of the palms is throwing down his ultimate challenge here. What think you? Hosanna or humbug?

I am the life.

On Palm Sunday, we can look back to John the Baptist, and see Jesus fulfilling his urgent demand: Prepare the way of the Lord. We can look further back to Zechariah and see Jesus fulfilling his prophecy about the humble king. What is there on Palm Sunday to look forward to?

It is the life yet to be lived, the protest yet to be made, the lonely act of courage, the challenge made to the city. And by 'city' we are meant to understand the powers that be, the establishment, the status quo. To follow the Palm Sunday man is to follow him as he questions political power, religious authority, and ultimately popular opinion, which always chooses Barabbas.

We'll hate it. But it is where God wants us to be. Out there, in public.

Blessed is He who comes in the Name of the Lord

A Palm Sunday litany

To those in the house of uncertainty
may He come as He came of old.
Not breaking down the door
but shedding light from within.

To those in the house of guilt
may He come as He came of old.
Not with the word that shrivels
but the Word that has wholeness at its centre.

To those in the house of fear
may He come as He came of old.
Not with the question that cannot be answered
but the question that opens windows.

To those in the house of defeat
may He come as He came of old.
Not with a thirst for explanation
but an explanation of tomorrow.

To those in the house of sorrow
may He come as He came of old.
Not with our helplessness
but death itself under His heel.

To those in the house of hunger
may He come as He came of old.
Not with only His arm and His hand
but with our awakened hearts.

To those in the house of hatred
may He come as He came of old.
Not with the violent remedy
but the flight of the dove.

To those in the house of exile
may He come as He came of old.
Not with the empty formula
but the promise of home.

To those in the house of chaos
may He come as He came of old.
Not with the bitter taste of failure
but the honey of hope.

Windows on the Passion

A meditation from Palm Sunday to Good Friday

Imagine that you are locked in a cell measuring six feet by four. You are all alone; there is nothing to look at but the four bare walls made of concrete blocks, plastered over with dull grey cement. Day after day, the unrelenting monotony of grey cement. Day after day, the same tasteless food is brought to you: bread, a boiled egg, slices of processed cheese.

Imagine the terror of being at the mercy of your captors. Imagine the terror at being at the mercy of yourself, of your memories, your fears and your nightmares. This is the terror which Brian Keenan, held hostage in Beirut, describes in his book *An Evil Cradling*: moving from states of calm to states of anguish, entering the panic of feeling that he has become unmanned by his solitary confinement. He describes himself as being in the charnel-house of history, like ash blown around by the wind. He is alone.

One day, one magical day, his jailers bring him a bowl of fruit: some nuts, a banana, cherries, a few small oranges. Keenan's reaction to the fruit is ecstatic: 'I lift an orange into the flat, filthy palm of my hand: the colour orange, my God the colour orange ...' The fruit mesmerizes him; he refuses to eat it. He needs to look at it, to feast his eyes on it. For days he sits and lets the sight and shape of the oranges tranquillize his terror: 'I sit', he writes, 'and look at the walls, but now this room seems so expansive, it seems I can push the walls away from me. I can touch them from where I am and yet they are far from me.'

What did Brian Keenan see when he looked at the oranges in his dark and stifling cell? They were more to him than an antidote to the monotony of grey cement: more than little cannonballs of juicy flesh, primed and ready to explode. They were, I'm sure, tokens of the sweetness of the world outside his cell: when he looked at them, did he not see the groves where they had ripened, sunlight on leaves, hillsides of blossom in the spring? He looked beyond the oranges to the place they had come from: he saw their liberty when they hung bravely on their branches: dancing in mid-air, harvesting light and warmth. He saw, maybe, when he looked at them, the man he had been before they bundled him into darkness and shackles, a dancing man, now fettered and enfeebled.

The glowing colours of the icons of the Passion bring us wider worlds. All icons, whether they are saints or Christ Himself or the Mother of God, heroes or heroines of legend, angels come to eat a simple meal with Abraham, apostles or defenders of the faith: all icons are pointers to the reality, or the mystery, which they suggest. They point beyond themselves; they are not images to be worshipped for themselves, they are not objects of 'religious art', and they do not invite our admiration or our approval. They invite us to pray, to meditate; their very simplicity deceives us. But when we learn to read the clues that they contain, we too can feel released from the grey monotony of our habitual thought-forms. Each icon is a window, a gateway to wider worlds.

The monks who painted icons were referred to not as painters but as writers, tellers of a story. Let's look at three icons of the Passion, three stories.

The entry of Jesus into Jerusalem, seated on a horse (donkeys were not animals familiar to the Russian monk), is an obvious starting point. Christ enters the city, the apostles following behind him. The crowd awaits him. There is a balance here: the Saviour between these two groups – but there is another balance, not seen but felt, not painted but etched into the awareness of us who look at this scene: the awareness that, immediately prior to his entry into Jerusalem, the Lord has raised to life his friend Lazarus. This is the first, express cause of the celebration which greets Jesus at the gates of the city: and we who watch know that the Lord is poised here, seated on a beast of burden, between the wonder of Lazarus' release from death and the greater wonder waiting to unfold – his rising, his coming forth from the tomb. When we look at the Palm Sunday icon, we are

meant to remember that this man is moving, purposefully, from one
victory to a greater victory.

You come to us, King Jesus,
without the ceremony of a king,
but seated on the back of a beast of burden.
You are the pied piper in reverse,
bringing children with you into the city,
bringing gleams of hope
into the eyes of the weary people;
where is your dignity, Prince of princes?
Where is your cavalcade?
Where is your official welcoming committee
of sober-suited councillors?
Where is your red carpet?
Surely not these jackets on the road?
Surely not these branches?

You come to us, King Jesus,
without the smug remoteness
of the conqueror: You bring excitement,
not rehearsed speeches.
You bring traders from their benches.
merchants from their counting-houses,
blacksmiths from their anvils,
the mason from his plumb-line.
You unbalance us, King Jesus.
You are bad for business.
You make us think
that there are other things to do, to be,
to be obsessed with.

You come to us, King Jesus,
without warning.
You do not give us time
to prepare a mask to meet you with.
You take us as you find us,

You are at ease with us
as if you'd known us for a thousand years,
as if you'd known us since the world began.
But we ... we still don't know
what to make of you.
We say 'Who is this?'

Who is this wandering preacher,
driving a wedge of delirium
into the heart of the business community,
into the seat of government,
into the headquarters of the military,
into the slums
and overcrowded tenements,
into the throne room of the palace,
into the hushed cathedral,
into the corridors of power,
into the banking-hall,
into the wilderness of affluence?
Who is this disturber of the peace,
this agent of pandemonium?
Who is this stranger
riding into town, with love and pity
and impatience flashing
from his every glance?

This is our God.
We have waited for him
that he might save us.
This is the Lord;
We have waited for him.
Let us be glad
And rejoice in His salvation.

How often, I wonder, are we poised between victory and victory?
Not often. We know too well what it is to be suspended between
partial gain and partial loss. Our nostalgia for a lost Eden is strong:

the place where everything is handed to us and nothing is demanded of us. Our longing for a Promised Land is so powerful: a place where there is no gap between promise and delivery, between hope and certainty. We are not at home with ambiguity – and yet, did we but realize it, ambiguity is a gift from God which invites us to be at home with the discipline of choosing, the dangers of freedom. If we disdain that gift, we opt for one desperate certainty or another – and there are dangers in both options. If we accept ambiguity, we choose the way of risk, the way of total loss or total gain. Is there any other way?

In most icons of the crucifixion, the scene is stripped down to its bare essentials. The crucified Christ dominates the icon, central, lifted high and clearly silhouetted against the open sky. To help us concentrate on him, the icon-writers ignore the thieves who were on his right and left, but they are suggested by the slanting bar on which the feet of Jesus rest, the bar which is always angled downwards from left to right, the up-tilted end pointing to the thief who said: 'Lord, remember me when you come into your Kingdom'. There is no crowd of spectators, no gambling soldiers: the witnesses to the suffering of the Son of Man are nearly always only Mary his mother and St John the beloved disciple. Sometimes they are joined by a holy woman standing beside Mary; and, behind John, the centurion who acknowledged Jesus as the son of God, traditionally called Longinus.

As if in counterpoint to the sparseness of the imagery presented to us, the liturgies which sing of the Cross are rich and densely populated with pictorial phrases and a profusion of descriptions. For example:

Shine Cross of the Lord,
shine with the light of thy grace
upon the hearts of those who honour thee.

Through thee our tears of sorrow
have been wiped away:
we have been delivered
from the snares of death
and have passed over to unending joy.

Thou art an invisible weapon,
an unbroken stronghold;
thou art the victory of kings
and the glory of priests.

Life-giving Cross, door to paradise,
succour of the faithful,
rampart set about the Church,

Christ our God,
of Thine own will
Thou hast accepted crucifixion,
that all mankind might be restored to life.

Taking the quill of the Cross
out of love for man,
in the red ink of royalty
thou hast signed our absolution.

Have you ever noticed, as you walk through the streets of a town
you think you know, that if you let your eyes be drawn upwards,
you may find inscriptions you weren't aware of on walls, plaques or
dates or names, linking a building to another time, another purpose?
How often do we miss these pointers? How glibly do we think that
streets exist only for us, only for the 'now' we occupy and inhabit?
How easily do we forget that streets and buildings have a history,
an explanation?

We need to notice in the icons of the Cross that there is a sign, a
pointer: not above the level of our eyes but below it, below the place
of execution, the icon shows us a skull, embedded in the darkness of
a cave or a tomb. Is this a piece of grisly embroidery, a comment on
death's prevailing power in our lives? Not really; the skull is there as
an explanation. This is no ordinary skull, but the remains of Adam,
who, legend has it, was buried in the place over which the Cross
was raised. When we have registered this, we have the meaning of
the icon: Christ is the one whose death on Calvary springs from the
first rebellion in Eden, and who reverses it. The Cross restores the
lost relationship:

Lifted high upon the Cross,
O Master, with Thyself,
Thou hast raised up Adam
and the whole of fallen nature.

The Tree of true life
was planted in the place of the skull
and upon it hast Thou,
the Eternal King,
worked salvation in the midst of the earth.

Hail! Cross of the Lord: through thee mankind has been
  delivered.

Faithful cross, above all other
    one and only noble tree,
none in foliage, none in blossom,
    none in fruit compares with thee:
Sweet the wood and sweet the iron,
and thy load, how sweet is thee.

Why does the Eastern Church feel free to use such extravagant
poetry, to multiply the images, the metaphors with which its worship teems? Why, more particularly, are these vivid word-pictures
heaped up around the Cross itself, like bouquets being thrown at the
feet of a singer by a rapturous audience?

Thou art our help,
Thou art the strength of Kings,
the power of righteous men,
the majesty of priests.

Thou art a sign of true joy.

Thou art the divine glory of Christ
who grants the world great mercy.

Hail! Guide of the blind,
Physician of the sick,
and resurrection of all the dead.

O Cross of Christ thou guide
of those who have gone astray, haven of the storm-tossed,
victory in warfare,
firm foundation of the inhabited earth.

Let all the trees of the wood rejoice,
for their nature is made holy by Christ
who planted them in the beginning
and who was outstretched upon the Tree.

The Cross is the guardian
of the whole earth.
The Cross is the beauty of the Church.
The Cross is the glory of angels
and the wonder of demons.

This is rapturous language: the Eastern Church dares to say what it feels, not just what it thinks. The Liturgy reacts to the Cross in the same way that Brian Keenan responded to the oranges in his cell, for in the Saviour's death the Orthodox see an entrance to a wider world. They see expansion, release, freedom for the captives. We are all prisoners, to some extent: the prisoners of our past, our failures, our distance from God. Our sense of restraint stifles the exultant shout of those who see in Calvary that the prisoner of Pilate is the one who frees us from our sin.

There is another strand to this: Good Friday is a sombre day, and the services are solemn and subdued. There are 12 readings – lengthy readings – from the Gospels. And there is this famous prayer:

Today He who hung the earth upon the waters is hung upon the Cross. He who is the King of the angels is arrayed in a crown of thorns. He who wraps the heaven in clouds is wrapped in the purple of mockery. The Bridegroom of the Church is transfixed with nails. The Son of the Virgin is pierced with a spear.

And then, immediately after this catalogue of what we did to the Christ, the Liturgy goes on to say: 'Thy Cross, O Lord, is life and resurrection to thy people; and putting all our trust in it, we sing to Thee, our crucified God: Have mercy upon us.'

'We sing to Thee, our crucified God ...' Just as the painted icons lead to prayer and meditation, the Cross itself leads to prayer and worship. The Cross itself is an icon. The One who hangs upon it is an icon. These are not my words, they are the words of St Paul: 'the god of this world has blinded the minds of those who do not believe, to keep them from seeing the light of the gospel of the glory of Christ, who is the likeness of God'. The word 'likeness' is the Greek word, *eikon*.

There is one more reason, I think, why the Eastern Church sings the Cross. Rabindranath Tagore, in his book *My Reminiscences*, comments on the difference in the attitude to singing between his native India and a European country like Britain. In India, he says, 'even our best singers cannot hide their sense of effort: the receptive portion of our audience have nothing against keeping the performance up to standard by dint of their own imagination'. In Britain, he finds something quite the opposite: here, we demand a faultless performance: 'There is no allowance for any weak spot in the singer's voice'. And he concludes: 'Our connoisseurs are content if they hear the song; in Europe they go to hear the singer'.

The Eastern Church sees Christ, obedient unto death, marooned on Calvary, exiled from both earth and heaven, and they see him there, singing the Lord's song in a foreign land. They enlarge that song, they add to it, they respond to it as if on rolling waves of words and tidal liturgies of acclamation – as if Jesus were the precentor, giving out the line, and the song is taken up and amplified.

We in the West have not learned that kind of freedom. We go to hear the singer. When the singer is dumb before us, clenched in the grip of agony, we don't know how to be rapturous. The bouquets wither in our hands. We may be shocked, even, to consider that there is another response to the Cross than our muted heaviness. The Cross is itself an icon, a window into the heart of God.

The third icon is the icon of the descent into hell. The Risen Lord, before his triumph is greeted by the women who come to the tomb

92

with spices, enters the prison-house of death to rescue and lift up those who have lain captive in the grey land of shadows: Adam, Eve, David, Solomon, John the Baptist, the church of yesterday awaiting its reprieve. Christ in a bright robe, garlanded in an almond-shaped blaze of gold, reaches out his arm to clasp the arm of Adam. We have come full circle now: not just in the Redeemer's mission of mercy but also in our short journey from our starting point with the oranges in Brian Keenan's dingy cell which brought close to him the fervent brightness of which he had been starved in his captivity, and gave him hints of wider worlds where light and space and freedom lie aplenty. Christ, brilliant in red, invades the greyness of death.

The sermon by St John Chrysostom, which forms part of the Easter vigil of the Orthodox Church and which is read every Easter, says it all:

> If anyone is devout and loves God, let them delight in this beautiful and radiant festival. If anyone wearies with long fasting, let them now receive payment. If any have worked from the first hour, let them receive today their just reward. If any waited till the third hour, let them keep the feast with thanksgiving. If any have come at the sixth hour, let them have no misgivings, for they shall assuredly lose nothing. If any have delayed till the ninth hour, let them draw near without fear. If any have waited even until the eleventh hour, let them not be afraid because of their lateness, for the Master, who is generous, will receive the last even as the first. Let none fear death, for the death of the Saviour has set us free. He has destroyed death by being captive to it. He, by descending into hell, made hell captive. Hell was angry when it tasted of his flesh. It was angry, for it was abolished. It was angry, for it was mocked. It was angry, for it was slain. ... O Hell, where is thy victory? Christ is risen, and thou art cast down. Christ is risen, and the demons have fallen. Christ is risen, and the angels rejoiced. Christ is risen, and life reigns.

Which Dish?

A reflection for Maundy Thursday

*'The one who has dipped his hand
in the dish with me will betray me'*

It is obvious, from what the Gospels tell us, that Jesus' talk about his betrayal, and how close his betrayer was to him, puzzles the disciples. 'Lord, who is it?' they ask. Jesus does not give them a name. He indicates who He means by giving Judas a morsel of bread, or meat – and even then the disciples react according to their smaller preoccupations. They think the words 'Do what you must do' refer to Judas using the common purse to lay in provision for the feast or giving charity to the poor.

We are there at that table. The gulf between Master and disciples is immense. The Master is talking about matters of life and death – his life and his death – and the disciples are thinking about a trip to Tesco or Asda. The gulf between Master and disciples is as wide, sometimes, as the gap between poetry and prose, the difference between a roaring Atlantic and the puddles where we stamp our feet to make a tiny splash. The challenge to the Church, need it be said, is to get back to that Atlantic wideness, depth, immensity and power. If only that immensity of power could come back to drench our ecclesiastical agendas and even our private ones too.

Don't let's be preoccupied with small things. And yet, this Maundy Thursday, I find myself preoccupied with something you may feel is trivial and of no account: yet, when I read the other day what John's Gospel tells us happened in the Upper Room, I found myself asking this question, about the morsel that was dipped into the dish and given to Judas. What dish? What dish did Jesus dip a piece of bread in to give to His friend, His enemy?

Let us make no mistake about it: I feel that whatever Jesus does here, as whatever else he does during Holy Week, is saturated with the significance he puts on it. His parables are not just words. They are physical. He is no longer telling stories about himself, he is telling the story of himself, and we have to watch each word and ponder every action, for they change places. Some of his actions are the last word on the matter, some of his words have the force of foundations that are pile-driven under the life of the Church, set there to undergird what we will do in his absence. The code is given to us. All we have to do is break it.

For example, the entry into Jerusalem is one of his most unforgettable sermons; the Redeemer preaching peace by coming to the city as a man of peace. But there's much, much more than that in the Palm Sunday story. I didn't notice what this was until I saw, one day, in Crete, a donkey's exhaustion as it carried a huge load of firewood down a dusty street. 'How can that poor beast carry such a weight?' I thought. And then I wondered: how much does a man weigh? And how even was that street? And he came into the city, trusting himself to a donkey to carry him. And he looks at us, knowing our strength is not that impressive and how shaky our balance is, and yet he twists this beast of burden, the Church, to carry the weight of his mercy and compassion, his forgiveness and tender love.

The code is given to us. All we have to do is break it. Will we ever know how he took bread and broke it and gave it to his friends in that Upper Room? Did he break the piece of matzo, the unleavened bread, delicately? Or did he close his fist around it and crumble it? Every Sunday when I brush crumbs away from my Communion service book, I realize that the Incarnation isn't tidy. I have domesticated this Christ and reduced Him to a still pool whose surface is unruffled, and the Atlantic surge of his authentic power comes roaring back and breaks in rolling waves against me.

The code is given to us. All we have to do is break it. He gives a morsel of bread to Judas, after he has dipped it in the dish. What dish?

If this was a Passover meal – and there may be some doubt about that – there were several dishes on that table. The lamb; the bowl of salt water, the reminder of the tears shed in Egypt and the waters of the Red Sea; the dish of bitter herbs, the sour taste of slavery in Egypt; the paste made of apples, dates, pomegranates and nuts, which brings to mind the clay which the Hebrew slaves in Egypt had to fashion into bricks.

What dish will he dip the bread in, and what will that say about him? What will that say about Judas, who is given it? What will it say about us, who watch this moment, so poignant and heavy-laden with bitter-sweet finality? Do we want him to give to Judas bread that is smeared with mud? Judas, you are dust, and to dust you shall return? Judas, you are still a slave in my eyes? I have not liberated you, so stay in your prison-house of small preoccupations, small greeds, small calculations? Wouldn't it be easy to hate this Judas, and not only to hate him but also to show you hate him?

I don't believe the Master sank to the level of that mean contempt. I, who betray him so often, cannot bear to think that he has contempt for me, the contempt I deserve. I cling to the thought that he has only love, the love I don't deserve.

What dish does he dip the bread in? The bitter herbs? The sour taste of slavery? I have to reject the notion that we are looking at slavish values here: as if Jesus is helpless, bound for the Cross after the manner of one who has no option, no alternative; as if Judas is chained to his destiny, bound to be a betrayer, condemned to his conduct, the prisoner of his smallness. If Jesus gave bitter herbs to Judas, he was elevating slavery into an inescapable condition – and I cling to the thought that Jesus never gave slaveries such dignity or worth. He loosed the chains of every slavery, be it someone's blindness and their bondage to the dark, or their lameness and bondage to disability, or their grief and their bondage to despair, or their sins and their bondage to their past. Does he not look at Judas, even now, and try to show him that he is free not to betray him? Does he not look at us and challenge us: do you love your slavery more than my freedom? I cling to the thought that Jesus says to Judas: you are sitting beside me, but you are a million miles away from me, and yet you are free to turn to me again and really be by my side.

What dish? Can you see his hand dip a piece of bread into the salt water, the tears of travail, and then give that morsel to Judas?

'See, Judas,' his hand says more eloquently than any words, 'I am giving you my sorrow.' There is more rebuke in sorrow than torrential anger, blame or accusation. There is more power in a look of sorrow than in a thousand speeches. And yet, don't let us narrow down this moment to the status of being a private transaction of regret between two men, as if Christ were near to indulging for a second his own, hidden grief. The pounding of the Atlantic tides comes back to flail and drench that little dish that sits on this table. For it is the tears of Israel that lap its sides, and the tears of a nation and its long history of struggle and its love/hate struggle with its own identity as chosen race, rebellious race, child and orphan. It's the tears of the nation that has known God's particular and pointed favour, and God's weariness and exasperation: the tides of faithfulness and faithlessness alike.

Here, in miniature, as a dewdrop can hold the sun's light, a piece of bread baptized in salt holds centuries of longing, wistfulness, stern devotion and fitful dreaming, pain and regret: regret for what has been, regret for what cannot be. And Jesus dipped a piece of bread in the dish and gave it to Judas. The bread was Jesus' sorrow for all that Israel yearned for but could never get: a Messiah with empires of supremacy to build, a Messiah reaping the harvest of unconquerable might, not a poor man who attaches significance to the crumb we offer him as though they were his longed-for banquet.

From Here to There

A Good Friday prayer

Where the long hard road to that desolate place, the Place of the Skull, is walked again, and where we know those who walk there by names we borrow from you, Jesus the Hunted, Jesus the Mocked, Jesus the Rejected:

Jesus, you are there.

Where the difficult road is taken, no bargain struck with the second-best, no short-cut to the shining prize:

Jesus, you are there.

Where the road dips down, the sun blotted out and the valley becomes a no-man's-land or, worse by far, a no-God's-land:

Jesus, you are there.

Where the road is the route to the way less travelled, the risky way, the creative path, the daring idea, the breakthrough of light:

Jesus, you are there.

Where the road is bruising and a trail of tears, the signposts blank and the maps all fail:

Jesus, you are there.

Where glory shines in the shuttered heart,
where the scales fall from awakened eyes,
where mercy and truth speak words of gentle power and You are
known again in the breaking of bread and our hearts burn within
us, Christ of Emmaus, Teacher who teases a song from the abyss,
Mender of broken Hallelujahs:

Jesus, you are there.

Dry-Shod above a Sea of Doubts

A prayer for Good Friday

Lord Jesus, we watch you now
As time is running out for you.
As Judas smiles and hides from you his lostness.
As Jerusalem goes about its business, unaware
that it is washed with tears.
As faithful men make plans to do a faithless thing
to you.
Lord Jesus, you walk towards the cross
as you alone could walk, dry-shod
above a sea of doubts and rolling tides of fear,
sure-footed among everything that threatens to unbalance you,
   a dancer,
knowing every step by heart.

For it is your heart you listen to,
the beating heart of love,
the tender heart of mercy,
the surrendered heart of obedience.

Lord, as we watch with you
we gain from you.
Our dreams of ease and painless struggle fade away.
Our dreams of straight, uncomplicated roads
dissolve and vanish.
Our dreams of living at no great cost to ourselves
creep out of sight
and out of mind.

Lord, in your mercy,
Save us from longing for these dreams again.

Let us watch with You, Watch-man of God.
As we see you walk towards the cross,
              let us walk with you.
As you face the suffering that lies before you,
              so let us face our moments,
                    our hours,
                          our days
of ultimate demand
        in the light of your eternity,
              your serenity,
                    your clarity.

Christ of the Scars

Intercessions for Good Friday

Christ of the scars,
into your hands we place
the wounded, the hungry,
and the homeless.

Receive them in love,
wounded one of the father.

Christ of the scars,
into your hands we place
the bereaved and the deserted,
the betrayed and the embittered.

Enfold them in tenderness,
wounded one of the father.

Christ of the scars,
into your hands we place
the children who are not wanted,
and those who suffer abuse,
be it mental or physical.

Shelter and shield them,
wounded one of the father.

Christ of the scars,
into your hands we place
those crushed by disappointment,

and those for whom life
has shown its cruellest side.

Heal and give hope,
wounded one of the father.

Christ of the scars,
into your hands we place
the frightened, the unfree,
the ones who wake each day
with dread, the restless
and those who have forfeited
their peace of mind.

Soothe and secure them,
wounded one of the father.

Christ of the scars,
into your hands we place
any who carry today the burden
of their wrong-doing.

Release them,
wounded one of the father.

Amen.

A Time for Silence

A meditation for Good Friday

Now Jesus stood before the governor; and the governor asked him, 'Are you the King of the Jews?' Jesus said 'You say so.' But when he was accused by the chief priests and elders, he did not answer. Then Pilate said to him, 'Do you hear how many accusations they make against you?' But he gave him no answer, not even to a single charge, so that the governor was greatly amazed.

Now at the festival the governor was accustomed to release a prisoner for the crowd, anyone whom they wanted. At that time they had a notorious prisoner called Jesus Barabbas. So after they had gathered, Pilate said to them, 'Whom do you want me to release for you, Jesus Barabbas or Jesus who is called the Messiah?' For he realised that it was out of jealousy that they had handed him over. While he was sitting on the judgment seat, his wife sent word to him, 'Have nothing to do with that innocent man, for today I have suffered a great deal because of a dream about him.' Now the chief priests and the elders persuaded the crowd to ask for Barabbas and to have Jesus killed. The governor again said to them, 'Which of the two do you want me to release for you?' And they said 'Barabbas'. Pilate then said to them, 'Then what should I do with Jesus who is called the Messiah?' All of them said, 'Let him be crucified!' Then he asked, 'Why, what evil has he done?' But they shouted all the more, 'Let him be crucified!'

Matthew 27:11–23 (NRSV)

Lamb of God, you take away the sin of the world.
Receive our prayer:
Word of the Father,
Father of all.

ALL   Strengthen us, Lord.

Lamb of God, you take away the sin of the world.
Grant us your peace:
Word of the Father,
Fisher of men.

ALL   Strengthen us, Lord.

By your human birth and your dire poverty, by your fastings and
your temptations, by your distress and anguish of soul, and by all
your pain:
Word of the Father,
Fisher of men.

ALL   Strengthen us, Lord.

By your agony, by your bonds and insults, by your scourging and
your crown of thorns, by your nailing to the cross:
Word of the Father,
Fisher of men.

ALL   Strengthen us, Lord.

By your wounds and your bitter death, by your descent from the
cross and your resting in the grave:
Word of the Father,
Fisher of men.

ALL   Strengthen us, Lord.

By your resurrection and your last days on earth, by your ascension and your reigning in power, by your continual intercession and by your return in glory:
Word of the Father,
Fisher of men.

ALL   Strengthen us, Lord.

May your willing acceptance of death reveal the mystery of your love for us; may your tears soothe our pains and our griefs; may your broken body and your blood poured forth be the food of our eternal life:
Word of the Father,
Fisher of men.

ALL   Strengthen us, Lord.

Almighty God, we pray you by the Passion of Your beloved Son to help us in all our trials and to be the strength for our human weakness, through Christ who lives and reigns for ever. Amen.

No Answer

A meditation for Good Friday

'But he gave him no answer, not even to a single charge, so that the governor was greatly amazed.'

> 'What language shall I borrow,
> To praise Thee, heavenly Friend,
> For this thy dying sorrow,
> Thy pity without end?'

The governor 'marvelled greatly', as the King James version of the Bible puts it. We don't often credit Pilate with a sense of wonder. We are more anxious to lay on Pilate the hesitations of us all, the indecisions of us all, the avoidance strategies of us all. But Pilate's sense of wonderment is significant and revealing.

We read that Jesus was silent before Pilate. 'He did not answer.' It's feasible, it's more than likely, that Pilate was also silent before Jesus. And when the governor's silence, born of wonder, rises to match the silence of the Saviour, then we know that we are moving out of interrogation into dialogue. Not just a meeting of men, but a meeting of minds. Not just a confrontation between the procurator and the prisoner, but a subtle change in the nature of that confrontation.

When we read that the governor 'marvelled greatly', we can be sure that the prisoner is reaching him at a level far above, or far beyond, the level of speech. Can we borrow something here from the governor? His marvelling, his musing, his mute acknowledgement that here, before him, is someone who makes him pause and plays a little havoc with his grasp of what is going on? Pilate, in that moment when you marvel, you are very nearly what you long to be again: a man. A pure and simple man, the man you left behind when you became a civil servant of the Roman Empire and accepted the responsibility of being governor. On that day, a little, or a lot, of the 'you-ness' of you vanished into the administrator, the planner, the official, the representative, the consul-general, the commissioner, the functional agent, the statesman, the commander, the coordinator. There's no need to go on. This is your moment, Pilate, to reclaim your lost past. Indeed, he's nearly there: 'he marvelled greatly'.

And in that moment, Pilate, who according to outward evidence is the jailer, the judge and the jury of the man who stands before him, becomes the pupil. The captive has captivated him. They have brought Jesus here to stand before him in chains, out of the Garden of Gethsemane into the guardroom – and yet Jesus has worked a little miracle again. He has brought the governor out of himself. For a moment, maybe. But a moment is enough. There is a ripple of light. For a second or two, maybe longer, these two are locked into a constructive dialogue: the dialogue of their silences.

There is a part of this act of worship in which a searching dialogue takes place: the Reproaches of the Cross. 'What have I done to you?' asks the liturgy. 'I led you forth out of Egypt, and delivered you by the waters of baptism, but you have prepared a Cross for the Saviour.' And we answer, shame-faced, in abasement: 'Holy God, Holy and mighty, Holy immortal One, have mercy upon us'. We have nowhere to run to. We are just like Pilate: we are locked into our problem. He is locked into the mind-set, the attitude, the strait-jacket of his authority and his role. He must be the governor, and yet Jesus offers him liberation: the healing, releasing power of marvel. Wonder.

And we, on this Good Friday, can feel locked into our role. We are helpless bystanders, spectators at an outrage we cannot prevent. For sure, shame and abasement are our only proper response. I dare to imagine that Jesus wills it otherwise. Today, again, he wills us into dialogue with him. It's not the dialogue of the helpless prisoner speaking to the powerless observers but the dialogue of the free man who wants us to be free too. We don't worship in this way today to wallow in our all-too-human failures. We worship in this way today to welcome His sublime and searching liberation. For, just as Jesus coaxed Pilate, for a moment, out of his governor's uniform and invited him to meet him as a man, so too the Lord – this is His saving work – invites us out of our self-inflicted defeats, our self-obsessed paralysis, our self-conscious awareness of how much we have failed him, into a dialogue, the dialogue of wonder.

If we can't relate to him in words, He makes it possible to relate to Him in silence. Strike a match: the noise it makes is almost infinitesimal, but it echoes all the same with clumsy thunder. But the sun rises in its splendour, silently, and bathes the world with light. And so too does the wonder of the love of God rise up and reach us, at a level above or far beyond the realm of speech: in the deepest levels of our being, where we are most inarticulate anyway, and all we are able for, all we are open for, all we are desperate for is a ripple of light.

Let us pray

Let us pray for the one holy, catholic and apostolic church of Christ throughout the world. For its unity in witness and service; for all church leaders and ministers and pastors, and the people they serve; for all Christians in this community, for those about to be baptized or confirmed, that God will keep the church in faith, increase it in love and preserve it in peace.

Jesus, one and only Son and Lamb of God the Father, you poured out the wine of your blood to buy us from death. Shield us, encircle us each day, each night, each light, each dark.

Let us pray for this church that God may strengthen his people here in the life of the baptized, embolden them to declare the gladness of the Gospel by the words of their mouths and by the actions of their hands. May this building be a hospitable space, and may it stand as a sign of your Spirit at work in the world and as a witness to our Lord and Saviour Jesus Christ.

Eternal God, by your Spirit the whole body of your faithful people is governed and sanctified. Receive our prayers which we offer before you for all members of your holy Church, that in our vocation and ministry we may truly and devoutly serve you, through our Lord and Saviour Jesus Christ.

Into the dangers, toils and snares of humanity, O Lord, you entrusted your only Son. You honoured our dust by the mystery of the angel's words to Mary, when heaven told her she was chosen to be the bearer and deliverer of heaven's purpose. You honoured our dust by giving Jesus to be born for us, that He might walk towards us with impatient love, that he might walk before us and be the Shepherd calling us by name, calling us into community, calling us to serve as his church.

We did not choose to be your heralds and to be your defenders. You chose us. A great mystery is your church. Nor did you choose us because we are a great people: it is clear for anyone to see that we are the least of all people. You have set your love upon us because you love us. A great mystery is your church. You died on Calvary to rise again and to reign. And we are buried with you in the waters of baptism that with you we might rise to newness of life. We are already dead, and our lives are hid with you. The undertakers have been and gone for us. Our citizenship is already in heaven. We are just your ambassadors here to represent you to a fallen world. So keep us, each of us to serve you as you deserve. God grant us wonder in that service, lively imaginations to thrill at the stars we cannot see, and feel the ripple of far-off distant oceans, through Jesus Christ our Lord.

King of the Friday

A meditation for Good Friday

O King of the Friday
who was stretched out on the Cross,
O Lord who did suffer
the bruises, the wounds, the loss,
may some fruit from the tree
of your passion
fall on us this day.

O Son of the tears
who was pierced for us,
may your cross be our shield
this day.

O Healer of souls and bodies
who made yourself small
and of no account,
let the shadow of Calvary
not darken our vision but deepen our faith this day.

When he saw that the sun had hidden its rays and that the veil of
the Temple was rent as the Saviour died, Joseph of Arimathaea
went to Pilate, and pleaded with him and cried out:

give me that stranger
who since his youth
has been a wanderer.

give me that stranger
upon whom I look with wonder
seeing him a guest of death.

give me that stranger
whom envious men
drove out of the world.

give me that stranger
that I may bury him in a tomb,
the one who has nowhere
to lay his head.

Night falls in the city.
The lamps still flare
in the Governor's windows.
He has received despatches from Rome,
to which the Senate demands an answer
by return. He will have to be up
Until 2 or 3 in the morning, dictating to secretaries.
The city is quiet.
The Governor rubs his eyes;
somehow
he cannot forget the prisoner
to whom today he gave a Latin name :
Iesus Nazarenus Rex Iudaeorum,
Jesus the Nazarene, King of the Jews.

'Scroll 5', he mutters.
The secretary prepares to write.
'Begin as follows:
This afternoon, the execution of an imposter.
a trouble-maker from the Galilee.

We have quelled the prospect of an uprising
and peace and good order have returned
to the streets. Jerusalem is secure.
Please be aware that I shall need extra troops
if such a situation were to arise again.
The army here is stretched
to breaking point.'

Sleep well, Pilate.
He is beyond your legions
and the centurions now.
He is beyond the scourge and the nails.
He is free to wreak havoc
wherever His Name is spoken.

The Above and the Beneath

A meditation for Good Friday

Joseph Parker, minister of the City Temple in London more than a century ago, was one of those preachers who possess an artistry with words. This is his picture of Jesus:

> an eye that changed from pity to judgment and from judgment to pity with startling rapidity, a voice in which thunders were chained and all the mysteries of music hidden, a voice marvellous: now so like other voices that it moved no sense of wonder, and now so unique that all other voices sounded shallow and commonplace as compared with its compass and solemnity. A strange Man, now shrunk from life, a mountain on fire, now sought as a garden of delight in which palms grew for wounded hearts and flowers bloomed that were fit for festivals of unutterable joy.

We remember today when that voice, the 'voice in which thunders were chained and all the mysteries of music hidden', first began to speak. It was when He heard that John the Baptist had been arrested, arrested for denouncing the loose morals of the court, arrested for criticizing Herod. When John was silenced, Jesus began to speak. He began to be the messenger, the interpreter. To say He was one in ten thousand would be to belittle Him. He is alone, supreme, the interpreter: 'the one who comes from above', writes St John, 'is above all. The one who is of the earth belongs to the earth and speaks about earthly things.'

Jesus brings together the above and the beneath. He speaks both languages: the language of the most High and the language of the most hurt, the language of the searching Father and the language of the lost child, the language of love and the language of longing.

And today we want to silence Him, to play the king who stopped the mouth of John the Baptist and shut him up in prison, to end the dialogue because it was too exacting, 'Forgive your brother seventy-seven times', He said. We couldn't cope with love's arithmetic. 'Love your enemies', He said. We couldn't cope with love's geography: crossing all borders, disdaining all boundaries. 'Judge not', He said. We couldn't cope with love's authentic logic. We tried to silence Him. And He said: 'Father, forgive them, for they know not what they do'.

He is never more surely, more emphatically the Interpreter than when He is on the Cross. Today He is the bridge which is strong enough to carry the love of God to us, the bridge which is strong enough to carry our human griefs to God. As the Scottish Episcopal Liturgy of 1982 has it: 'In Christ your Son our life and yours are brought together in as wonderful exchange. He made His home among us that we might forever dwell in You.' As the Orthodox song of the God-man puts it:

as man he went to the wedding at Cana of Galilee, and as God he changed the water into wine, as man he slept in a boat, and as God Her commanded the wind and the sea and they obeyed him. As man He wept for Lazarus, and as God He raised him from the dead. As man He rode on a donkey but they acclaimed Him as God. As man he was crucified and as God He brought the good thief into paradise with him. As man he tasted the vinegar and gave up the spirit and as God he blocked out the sun and made the earth tremble. As man He was placed in the sepulchre and as God He conquered Hell and freed its prisoners.

King o the Daw

An Easter hymn

(tae the tune 'Martyrs')

His face it wis sae doonward bent
An laich He cast His ee,
O sic a wecht o dool He kent,
O sic a draucht o dree.

It wis a mirksome, eerie day
He made for Calvary,
An cairried aa yon wecht o wae
Tae set His kindred free.

It wis a mornin bricht wi dyowe;
Wi saws the weemin came –
An faar He'd lain wis teem an howe,
An He wis lichtly gane.

*The Scots word 'daw' means 'dawn' – and here the weight of grief
and fear that Jesus experienced on the way to Calvary to bring freedom is contrasted with the bright morning when the women came to
the tomb and found Jesus gone.*

Close Enemies

An Easter poem

There were three men in that country
Who walked and slept in fear.
Each saw his own sweet fantasies
In front of him appear.

For Caesar, Pilate held the rule
And beat a martial drum.
Each loyal Jew was ready for
The day of wrath to come.

In purple and in jewels bright
Sat Herod on his throne
He was the landlord poor and weak
Of all the might of Rome.

And Caiaphas the Temple Mouse
Who prayed with open eyes:
And Caiaphas with cunning says
'Find me a man that dies'.

There were three men in that country
Three lonely men of power
Close enemies and distant friends
Who waited for their hour.

There was one man in that country
One daring, dreaming man
Their flags and thrones and prayers too
Could not destroy the plan.

The Day the Lord has Made

An Easter prayer

Lord, this is Your day.
The day of light, we would remember that this is the day of
Resurrection:
a day for desert hearts to throw aside the taste and texture of the
wilderness,
a day for weariness to be met and soothed and bound up gently with
the healing of the Gospel,
a day for the bracing and clear challenge of God to reach us wherever
we are stifled, cribbed, cabined or confined.

This is Your day, Lord.
You will forgive our sins if we want to be forgiven:
You will speak to us if we will listen:
You will heal us if we are willing to be healed:
You will give us the Morning Star, if we crave Your glorious hope:
You will reach down to us, if we wish to be lifted up:
You will reach out to us, if we admit that we need You:
You will make Your home in us, if we make room for You:
You will hear us, if we make the effort to make our requests in true
humility and in that blessed poverty whereby we do not have to
pretend to be self-sufficient:
you, Friend of Sinners, Physicians of Souls, will seek us out and find
us, if we want to be found.

Lord, have mercy upon us
Christ, have mercy upon us
Jesus, Bread of life,
Jesus, Good Shepherd,

Jesus, Lamb of God,
Jesus, name above every name, may Your risen power so move our hearts and hands that we may know again beyond all doubting that on this Your day Your will for us is that we should know Your love and pity, Your health and purpose. Your victory. Amen.

The Infinite Treasure of Renewal

An Easter prayer

Loving God,
Now the breadth and depth and cost of Your love are known.
In the birth of Jesus,
Heaven and earth fuse in a child;
You draw back the veil of separation
And touch the here and now with the eternal:
Christ takes the mantle of our humanity:
Loving God,
We worship You.

Gracious Father, in the death of Jesus Christ Your Son,
Our sin and Your mercy embrace:
You cast light into the darkness of our deeds,
And offer to us the hand of forgiveness,
Gracious Father,
We worship You.

Eternal God,
In the resurrection of Jesus,
The infinite treasure of renewal is seen,
The breaking of the spiral of despair and desolation is known,
And assurance for the future is found,
Christ is risen to life again!
Eternal God,
We worship You.

Loving God,
We sing to You with cheerful voice,
We come into Your presence and rejoice,
For now,
The depth and breadth and cost of Your love is known,
In Jesus Christ our Lord.

'Unless I see the marks of the nails on His hands ...'

God our Father,
We come before You now to confess
Our stubborn doubting –
Our troubled denial –
Our prideful disbelief –
For we, so often like Thomas,
Ask for proof,
Demand signs,
Search for evidence.

Lord, have mercy upon us
Christ, have mercy upon us.

Lord, have mercy upon us,
As we confess too that we have forgotten what He taught us,
We have been selfish – neglecting the needs of our neighbours,
We have spoken carelessly and in anger,
And caused hurt to families and friends.

Lord,
In Your great mercy and kindness,
Grant us Your forgiveness,
Heal our blindness,
Release us from the imprisonment of fear and doubt,
And help us to live as children of the resurrection
For the sake of Jesus Christ, our Risen Lord,
Who lives and reigns with You and the Holy Spirit,
One God, now and for ever,
Amen.

The Day Fresh Made

An Easter prayer

Bless to us, O God, this day, fresh made.
In the chorus of birds – bless us;
In the scent of blossoms – bless us,
In the wet grass and spring flowers – bless us;
Bless us and heal us,
For we come to You in love and trust.
We come to You in expectant hope.

We lift our hearts and voices to praise You, O God of the new day,
O God of new beginnings,
Remembering the newness You give to the world
Through the resurrection of Jesus Christ.

We lift our hearts and our voices to praise You –
Remembering that this is the new beginning of all time –
The hope for us all.

We lift our hearts and our voices to praise You, O Risen Christ,
Remembering
that Yours is the power that reaches all hearts,
that Yours is the sacrifice that challenges our indifference,
that Yours is the glory that spans the earth,
that Yours is the victory and the triumph.

Come Risen Christ,
and touch our hearts and lives –
Come in power and glory to all nations and make the kingdoms of
    this world
The Kingdom of God.

An Introduction to an
Easter Communion

The Lord be with you ...

It is truly right, our duty and our joy,
Always and everywhere,
To give You thanks
Almighty God, Heavenly Father,
For You are the source of all richness and blessing;
The fountain of all goodness and grace:

O God of new beginnings
We bless You and thank You
For the hope that is at the heart of Easter –
The light of resurrection flooding over the shadow of the Cross:
We bless You and thank You
For the light of resurrection scattering the shadows of our doubts
and uncertainties:

We bless You and thank You, Father,
For the faithful of every time and place
Who have inspired and influenced and enriched others
By living their lives for You,
In the radiance of Your rising,
And who now live with You in everlasting light and peace.
And so we join our voices,
And the struggle song of earth,
To the triumph song of heaven,
Praising You in the angels' hymn – Holy, holy, holy ...

Accept, Father, this offering of ourselves and our gifts.
Bless and use, we pray, all that we bring to You:
And grant that, blessed by You,
We may be a people of praise and power and light,
For the sake of Jesus Christ,
Who taught us when we pray to say – Our Father ...

Marching to a Different Drummer

A prayer for a centenary at Easter

This is a great day, a high day, a day for weary hearts to sing, a day for tired feet to dance again, a day for mortal, earthbound creatures such as we are to throw off the chains of care and the fetters of habit: for this is Your day, Lord of the rolling years; Your day, Christ of the shattered tomb; Your day, Spirit of change and movement and the liberation of everything and everyone that bears the stamp of dull defeat.

Fretting at the limits of time, we sense eternity can speak again to us; bound by the crushing weight of every human worry, fear, uncertainty and disappointment we feel unburdened here: not just in the shelter of these friendly stones around us, but in the space You, Christ of gladness, Christ of the morning, Christ of the new beginning, the space You have created by Your rising again.

We are in that space whenever we are met together, and whenever we are most alone. And yet we miss the gladness when our attention wavers: our concentration falters: we forget we're meant to be an Easter people and children of the Resurrection:

Lord, have mercy upon us
Christ, have mercy upon us
Lord, have mercy upon us.

Lord of the days that are past,
Lord of the days that are to be,

We pause now to let this special moment reach us: the moment when we thank You for a hundred years of working hard and playing hard; a hundred years of marching to a different Drummer. Behind us lie brave beginnings. Lord, let us be brave enough today to see that this centenary is a milestone, not a headstone.

Behind us, lives that were broadened, brightened, changed are woven into the story we are telling now, Lord. You are the One who changes us and keeps on changing us. Behind us, effort and energy have gone into the making of this glad occasion. Lord, keep us serving 'til the break of day.

Keep us marching to the different Drummer: the Jesus who breaks and remakes us, the King whose Kingdom rescues us from selfishness, isolation, despair and futility. Lord, keep us alert to the sound of His voice saying 'Follow me' to fishermen and to us; keep us by His side always, strong to defend the weak, brave to uphold the night, eager to take our stand for love's demanding task and love's own endless work:

> Lord, have mercy upon us,
> Christ, have mercy upon us,
> Lord, have mercy upon us.

May God in His goodness hear what our hearts are saying, and may He take us, shape us and direct us to go forward into His adventure with Him and for Him
Through Jesus Christ our Lord
Amen.

Footsteps in the Dew

A meditation for Easter Communion

Christ is risen!
The Lord is risen!

He is risen indeed!

Keep high holiday now
and be glad!
Now are all things filled with light:
Heaven and earth alike!
So let us bring to the Lord a song instead
of myrrh

Christ is risen!
The Lord is risen!

He is risen indeed!

An old Gaelic incantation reflects the commandment against the making of graven images: 'No smith shall make, no craftsman shall make, no mason shall make, no wright shall make gear nor tool, weapon nor device, tackle nor instrument ... to check you, enclose you, rend you, bridle you, there nor here, on earth or sea, here not yonder, down nor up, above nor below, in the sky above, in the deep beneath'.

This Easter Day we rejoice:

no smith, no craftsman
no nails from the white forge

no chains with links of bronze or iron,
no mason, no wright,
no stone, no cross of timber,
no device, no instrument,
to check you, enclose you,
rend you, bridle you
there not here
down nor up
above nor below

In the glory of the morning
in the blindfold of the dark
God has spared us,
He has helped us,
He has brought us to this hour,
some dragging their feet,
living the pain of the last step,
the next step.

'On the first day of the week, at the first sign of dawn, the women
went to the tomb ... Mary of Magdala, Joanna, Mary the mother of
James, and other women with them also.'

Some free as air,
blithe as birds in flight,
In colours of splendour

'As the women stood there, not knowing what to think, two men in
brilliant clothes suddenly appeared at their side.'

Some full of fear

'Terrified, the women lowered their eyes.'

Some possessed of calm certainty

'The two men said to them:
Why look among the dead for someone who is alive?

He is not here: He has risen.
Remember what He told you.'

Some sent to be heralds

'When the women returned from the tomb, they told all this to the
Eleven and to all the others.'

Some speechless, utterly unable to understand; some deaf, incapable
of receiving this information; some unready, some in denial.

'But this story of the women seemed pure nonsense, and they did not
believe them.'

Some wondering

'Peter, however, went running to the tomb.'

Some curious

'Peter bent down and saw the binding clothes but nothing else; he
then went back home, amazed at what had happened.'

Jesus, the splendour of the Father,
Jesus, brightness of eternal light,
Jesus, King of Glory,
Jesus, Good Shepherd,
Jesus, Shield of homesteads,
Jesus, True Physician,
Jesus, Most Powerful,
Jesus, Most Patient,
Jesus, Lover of Souls,
Jesus, Brother of the Poor,
Jesus, True Light,
Jesus, Joy of Angels,
Jesus, Teacher of the Evangelists,
Jesus, Light of Confessors,
Risen Lord, we praise you,

Glory to you, Conqueror of death
Glory to you, for the light
of your triumph is upon the earth
and the light of your victory
has shone into our hearts,
and with the choirs of heaven
we the citizens
of uncertain earth
break into song.
Great is the mystery of faith:
Christ has died
Christ is risen
Christ will come again.

Easter morning.
The floods of death have abated.
On the ark of His body
He has come to earth again,
to dry land,
and the tides of night
have been turned back,
and He has commanded
the angel of ravens
to announce Him:
The angel of doves
to carry the news of His triumph;
the angel of dawn
to banish the shadows.
He has told the women,
Mary of Magdala, Joanna,
Mary the mother of James,
'Go to your homes again,
go to your men
and your children.
Take up your lives.
I have gone beyond your anointing;
the spices are all redundant.

The bargain with night
has ended.
I have been to the forge
where the nails were struck,
and blessed it again.
I have been to the anvil
where the links of the chains
were cast, and blessed it again.
I have been to the forest
where the wood of the cross
was hewn,
and blessed it again.
I have been to the axe
that shaped the wood
and hallowed it, made it
as new.
I have been to the counting-house
where the thirty pieces of silver
were minted, and I have
purified it.
I have gone to the terror
and the hells of remorse,
the caves of shame
and the tears of the lost,
and I have bathed the faces
of those who wept
with a glory never seen
or felt on sea or land.'

Majesty, worship his Majesty,
Unto Jesus be all glory, power and praise.
Majesty, kingdom, authority
Flow from his throne unto his own, his anthem raise.
So exalt, lift up on high the name of Jesus.
Magnify, come glorify Christ Jesus the King.
Majesty, worship his Majesty,
Jesus who died, now glorified, King of all kings.

This is majesty,
this is kingdom authority,
that He should go down
to the depths to assert His power there;
but it is not the depths only,
nor the land of the dead only,
that He visits as a conqueror:
It is the past He is visiting,
with infinite mercy,
so that none who came before this Shining Day
might be forgotten, none abandoned,
none left outside.
All the way back to Adam himself,
the Redeemer travels to bring
the prisoners into daylight,
to include them in the commonwealth
of this Day's gladness.
He invades the land of death
and it is powerless to resist Him.

STANFORD: Te Deum Laudamus in B Flat
(Sung in English: 'We praise thee, O God')

Can we, dare we, believe He is not only Lord of the road not travelled yet, but also Lord of the road behind us, travelled badly?

Can we, dare we, believe that the Lord's descent – into the land of shadows, the Harrowing of Hell – is in reality an unmistakeable reassurance that He redeems the past as surely as He redeems what is, what shall be?

When He goes to the land of shadows to raise up fallen Adam, is He not also going to the past we've buried, the guilts we've hidden, the defeats we've suffered and can't forget?

His Lordship is a full Lordship. His healing power reaches back as well as forward.

You and I are the victims of time.

What is done is done. What is said is said.

But He is the Lord of time. The same yesterday, today and forever.
Change that: the same forever, today and yesterday. He is not the
victim of time.

> *Be still, my soul: thy God doth undertake*
> *To guide the future as he has the past.*
> *Thy hope, thy confidence let nothing shake;*
> *All now mysterious shall be bright at last.*
> *Be still my soul: the waves and winds still know*
> *His voice who ruled them while he dwelt below.*
>
> *Be still my soul: when dearest friends depart,*
> *And all is darkened in the vale of tears,*
> *Then shalt thou better know his love, his heart,*
> *Who comes to soothe thy sorrow and thy fears.*
> *Be still, my soul: thy Jesus can repay,*
> *From his own fullness, all he takes away.*

Blessed be your Name,
O Christ, Conqueror of death,
for the light of your triumph is upon the earth,
and the light of your victory has shone into our hearts,
to give the knowledge of the glory
and the power of God.

Blessed are you, Jesus.
Early in the morning
a voice in a guarded graveyard
and footsteps in the dew
declared that you had risen,
that you had come back
to those and for those
who had forgotten you,
Denied you, disowned you.
Hallowed be your Name.

Blessed are you, Jesus,
This is your morning,
your own third morning,
Blessed are you the First,
Blessed are you the Last.
Blessed is your Bethlehem
when you came to us
in the shroud of night.
Blessed is this morning
when you come back to us,
leaving your shroud behind.
Blessed is the fanfare
of your first coming,
the cry of Mary
stabbing the stillness
of night.
Blessed is your fanfare
now, silent, inescapable:
Footsteps in the dew.

Come now: come very close:
you that are far off and
you that are near:
you who laugh and dance in brilliance
and you whom many cares have overtaken:
you that have memorable things to do yet
and you that have only memories to feast on:
come close now
you that are ready to be captivated,
and you that have no mind to let
invading angels brighten up your tombs:
come close now,
read where He walks
read where He passes by
be ready to be breathless
when you see His footsteps in the dew.

Blessed are you, Jesus,
you are my song
In the house of night,
my shield against the quarrels.

Blessed are you
whose mercy guards the heart
in the panic of yes and no.
Blessed are you
who brings chains
out of the darkness.

Blessed are you, Jesus,
who have written your name
on the chaos.
Let each and all
be sheltered in the fortress
of your name.

Create the world again
and stand us up,
as you did before,
on the foundation
of your light.

Bring me back
me the wanderer
me the exile
me the fugitive.
Bring me back
to the homeland of my heart
where you are worshipped forever.

Awaken me to the mercy
of the breath
which you breathe in me.

Blessed is the name
of the glory
of your kingdom
forever and ever.

Today is for declaration.
A day for dwelling on
the gladness of surprise.
Christ has robbed the dark
of all its disguises.
A day for praising
the God whose pathway
is marked by
footsteps in the dew.
A day for praising life.

'Yes, he is here in this
open field, in sunlight, among
the few young trees set out
to modify the bare facts –
he's here, but only
because we are here.
When we go, he goes with us
to be your hands that never
do violence, your eyes
that wonder, your lives
that daily praise life
by living it, by laughter.
He is never alone here,
never cold in the field of graves.'

S. S. WESLEY: '*Blessed be the God and Father*'

Blessed be the God and Father of our Lord Jesus Christ,
Which, according to his abundant mercy, hath begotten us again
unto a lively hope by the resurrection of Jesus Christ, from the dead.
See that ye love one another with a pure heart fervently.
But the word of the Lord endureth for ever, for evermore. Amen.

Children of the Resurrection

An Easter Communion prayer

The Lord be with you
Lift up your hearts
Let us give thanks to our Lord God.

Let us give glory to God and thanks
for Christ behind us.

You enter, Jesus,
through the door of the past with your love and forgiveness.
You can enter where doors are closed,
and bring light and peace.
Come, Lord, and enter now
into the remembered and the forgotten
into the joys and the sorrows
into the regrets that wound us
into the places where, with hindsight,
we could have been sensitive, generous or gentle,
but we weren't.

Faithful Physician,
mend what we cannot mend;
change what we cannot change.
Let our blackest moments
yield to your timeless light,
so that what we cannot live with
is blessed into oblivion, and loses its power to blemish.

Let us give glory to God and thanks
for Christ before us.

We trust you, Jesus,
with our yesterdays.
We trust you for tomorrow.
You go before us.
Our deserts and our temptations
are familiar territory to you.
Lord of the turbulent sea,
the storms that capsize us are known to you.
Lord of the wilderness,
the loneliness we face at times is not new to you.
Lord of Gethsemane,
any cross we carry already has your fingerprints upon it.
Lord of Calvary, risen Lord, you have gone before us.
Remind us always that we are children of the Resurrection.

Let us give glory to God and thanks
for Christ beside us.

Born for us: Bethlehem child.
Baptized for us: pilgrim and teacher.
Betrayed for us: pawn in the power games.
Broken for us: man without sin
Buried for us: you really died that you might really rise.
We who are time-bound, fettered here to sign and symbol,
proclaim you, risen and glorious,
until you come again.

Until that day when the adoration of your people shall sing one song
We join our voices to the voices of those who sing already, Holy,
    Holy, Holy....

In your kindness send now, O God, your Spirit among us
that this bread may be for us
the Communion of the Body of Christ.
In your kindness send now, O God, your Spirit among us
that this wine may be for us
the Communion of the Blood of Christ.

And here we offer you ourselves,
our souls and bodies,
alone and in society;
here we offer you
our work, our worship,
our congregation, our community, our church.
We offer you the unyielding facts we wrestle with,
the dreams we reach for.
We offer you our brokenness and our wholeness.
Grant that what we offer here may be blessed and used and united with your
perfect working
Through Jesus Christ our Lord.

The Green Blade

An Easter broadcast

MUSIC   Toccata from *Symphony Number 5* by Widor

Voice: Sing, O heavens, for the Lord has done it!
           Sing to God, O Kingdoms of the earth!
           Christ is risen!
Response: He is risen indeed!

V: Christ is raisit!
R: Atweel He's raisit!

V: Let the heavens rejoice
           And let the earth be glad!
           For the Lord has shown strength with His arm,
           and trampled down death by death.
           Giver of life, O Christ our God.
R: Glory to You!

V: O Lord, our Resurrection and our Life
R: Glory to You!

V: Christ is risen!
R: He is risen indeed!

V: Christ is raisit!
R: Atweel He's raisit!

V: O Sing unto the Lord a new song!
           For He has done marvellous things.
           Let the sea roar, and the floods clap their hands;
           Let the hills sing for joy together!

| | Christ is risen! |
| R: | He is risen indeed! |

| V: | Christ is raisit! |
| R: | Atweel He's raisit! |

| V: | Christ is Risen! |
| R: | He is risen indeed! |

V: The day of life is here!
        Sing, Church of God!
        Exult with joy!
        Death is overthrown and Christ our God is risen,
        granting His great mercy to the world!
        O Lord, bright morning star,
        Alpha and Omega,
        first and last.
R: Glory to you!

V: This is the chosen Holy Day,
        the one King and Lord of Sabbaths,
        The Feast of feasts and the Triumph of triumphs:
        Christ is risen!
R: He is risen indeed!

V: Christ is raisit!
R: Atweel He's raisit!

MUSIC   'O Rejoice, that the Lord has arisen', the Easter Hymn
        from *Cavalleria Rusticana* by Mascagni

V: He for our sake that suffered to be slain
        And lyk a lamb in sacrifice wes dicht
        Is lyk a lyone rissin up agane
        And as a gyane raxit him on hicht:
        Sprungin is Aurora radious and bricht
        On Loft is gone the glorious Apollo,

The blisful day depairtit fro the nicht:
Surrexit dominus de sepulchro.

MUSIC   'Now Israel may say', Metrical Psalm 124

V: Heaven, rejoice.
          Earth, rejoice.
          All people rejoice.
          Everything that moves, stands, grows, breathes, rejoice.
          Let joy go down to where the roots of living things clasp
          the earth in secret.
          Let joy fling out along the trackless paths of space.
          O Christ of rising –
R: Glory to You!

V: Let nothing in the universe stand exempt from joy.
          Christ, King, Jesus rises.
          Rocks split before the explosive tomb, and the peal of
          His coming forth tears the darkness to shreds.
          O Christ of surprises –
R: Glory to You!

V: Light swells upon us like a giant beating his chest; and
          dark things,
          Shame and fear and guilt slink away before His incandes-
          cent flesh.
          We stand in a ring of fire.
          Christ is risen!
R: He is risen indeed!

V: Christ is raisit!
R: Atweel He's raisit!

V: The fo is chasit.
2nd V: The enemy is on the run.
V: The battell is done ceis.
2nd V: The battle's over.
V: The presone broken.

142

2nd V:	The prison shattered.
V:	The jevellouirs fleit.
2nd V:	The jailers fled.
V:	The weir is gon.
2nd V:	The war is finished.
V:	The feild is win.
2nd V:	The field is won.
V:	He has paid our ransom.

He has bought us
And bought our praise and gratitude.
We sing in our chains.
Heaven marries earth.
The light of Christ clothes us in splendour.
In the torrent of His radiance he burns out of darkness
like the midday sun.

MUSIC   Hymn: 'Now the green blade rises'

'Love lives beyond
The tomb, the earth, which fades like dew!
'Tis seen in flowers
And in the morning's pearly dew;
In earth's green hours
And in heaven's eternal blue.

'Tis heard in Spring
When light and sunbeams, warm and kind,
On angel's wing
Bring love and music to mind.

Love lives beyond
The tomb, the earth, the flowers and dew
I love the fond,
The faithful and the true.'

'Consider the lilies – they were Your little brothers,
Were they not – ?

Most gold and glad exactly
At Your dying time, their time for bravery,
And still their trumpet-mouths
Keep on announcing You: fanfares
For the Springtime of the heart
And Resurrection weather.'

MUSIC   ALLELUIA from South Africa. (*Touch the Earth Lightly,*
New Songs from Scotland)

Lord, who created man in wealth and store,
Though foolishly he lost the same,
Decaying more and more
Till he became
Most poor.
With thee
O let me rise
As larks, harmoniously,
And sing this day Thy victories;
Then shall the fall further the flight in me.

Taizé Chant: *Adoramus Te Domine*

V: We believe, O God of all gods,
         That You are the Eternal Father.

         Adoramus Te Domine

V: The Creator of the ends of the earth,
         The skies above, the wide rolling seas.

         Adoramus Te Domine

V: You gave to our bodies breath
         And to our souls their possession.

         Adoramus Te Domine

V: We believe, O God of gods,
           That You gave us Your beloved Son.

Adoramus Te Domine

V: Dying, he destroyed our death.
           Rising, he restored our life.

Adoramus Te Domine

V: We believe that He will come again,
           As tides ebb and flow,
           As moons wax and wane,
           So Your promise will be fulfilled.

Adoramus Te Domine

V: And death shall have no dominion.

Adoramus Te Domine

V: Though lovers be lost, love shall not.

Adoramus Te Domine

V: And death shall have no dominion.

V: Christ is risen!
R: He is risen indeed!

V: Christ is raisit!
R: Atweel He's raisit!

V: Christ is risen!
R: He is risen indeed!

V: The Gospel of the Resurrection;
           The Gospel of the God of life;
R: To shelter us, to keep up.

V: The Gospel of Christ our Light
R: The Holy Gospel of the Lord.

V: On the first day o the wik, i the gray of the mornin, they gaed oot tae the graff wi the spices they hed prepared. They faund the steen rowed awa frae the graff, an gaed in, but the bodie faundna they. They war ferliein sair what tae mak o it, whan aa o a suddentie, twa men in skinklin claes kythed aside them and said tae them, as they stuid there wi boued heids in unco dreid: 'What for seek ye the livin amang the deid? He isna here, he is risen!'
Christ is raisit!
R: Atweel He's raisit!

V: 'On the Sunday morning, very early, they came to the tomb, bringing the spices they had prepared. Finding that the stone had been rolled away from the tomb, they went inside, but the body was not to be found.

     While they stood utterly at a loss, all of a sudden, two men in dazzling garments were at their side. They were terrified, and stood with eyes cast down, but the men said 'Why search among the dead for one who lives? He is not here; He has been raised!'
Christ is risen!
R: He is risen indeed!

MUSIC   Hymn: 'Jesus Christ is risen today'

V: Morning has broken.
Christ is risen.
R: He is risen indeed!

V: Where shadows reigned
and hope fell silent,
God speaks a new word.
Where all seemed futile

God begins again.
Everything is changed.
Christ is Risen!

R: He is risen indeed!

V: Now the night is over
and the weeping of the generations
becomes the wedding feast
of now and every time to come.
God has kept the best wine
until last: after His life,
so full of vitality;
after His work of healing,
so rich with compassion;
after His days among us,
radiant with brightness;
after the long night of Gethsemane
and the deep dark of Calvary,
God gives us now
cause for joy,
reason for gladness;
He has taken Christ
from the narrow house of death
to set His feet
upon the high reaches of eternity.

Christ is risen!

R: He is risen indeed!

V: Christ, King, Jesus, rises.
He lives now not only
in the memory of things recalled
but in the moment accessible to us,
in the Now where life is,
in experience of grace.

He comes again to those who lost Him.
He comes again to those who forsook Him.
He comes again to those who avoided Him.
He comes again to those who betrayed Him.
He comes again to those who forgot Him.

We, who have done all these things, need to remember
Him, risen from the dead:
When the news comes that a friend has died, and one
more loneliness has come into our lives;
when faith is at its lowest ebb and our willpower is
paralyzed;
when we see a church which is no longer a house of
prayer but a warehouse, a store-room, an empty shell;
when we see a good person going through a harrowing
experience of suffering or setback, so that their
goodness seems to be mocked and made no account;
when the tired pilgrim looks ready to abandon the
pilgrim road;
when someone is at crisis point, and they have to
choose the way forward, and the way forward is the
hard way because standing still spells death, when grief
tightens its hold and will not let go,
when cherished dreams have crumbled into dust,
when the carefully laid plan is smashed to smithereens,
when we look for God and cannot find Him,
when we listen for His voice and all we hear is our own
heartbeat in the darkness,
when we see might triumph over right, and cruelty
having free rein, and lies have a field day,
when we face a blank wall and look behind us, to find a
cul-de-sac,
when we cannot pray and we cannot sing,
when there are more questions than answers,
when the anxieties of living seem to multiply beyond
our capacity to deal with them,
when we put time and energy into some endeavour only

to find that the outcome is a parody of what we looked
for,
when love reaches out and is rebuffed,
when love is not returned,
when love meets no response,
when the story seems ended and there is nothing to be
done; nothing to be done:

Then we need to remember him, risen from the dead.
And there are times when remembering Him, risen from
the dead, is as real as a handshake, as warm as kisses:
When the news comes that a friend has shaken off some
disaster and has begun to pick up the pieces again;
when we see grief being mastered and surely replaced
with resolution, bravery, determination;
when someone says 'Yes' to a challenge or a choice
which will take every ounce of their energy;
when we hear laughter coming back to someone's
repertoire of expression; when we listen to an old
person, or a young person, who has opted for defiance
instead of despair;
when a woman enters a church for the funeral of her
teenage son, killed in an accident, dressed in purple, a
bright scarf at her throat;
when someone faces pain or disability without self-pity;
when someone carries the agony of someone else
without looking for praise, when a glorious change
happens and someone leaves off complaining and
whining;
when a war of words stops, or a war of silences;
when a wrong is put right and a massive injustice is
dealt with;
when we shake off a poisoned attitude,
when we disdain revenge;
when we give up being haunted by a sense of inferiority;
when we stand on our own feet,
when we dismiss our pride and learn to apologize,

when a purpose comes back to rescue us from
aimlessness,
when we see that we are being shaken out of our
prejudices, and we know that God is behind it,
when we rise to some generosity of heart or spirit that
we never thought we were capable of,
when we can live with the memories instead of dreading
them,
when the past ceases to be a dead weight and failure
stops being the commanding factor,
when doors open that used to be shut,
when you know that it's all to play for and there is
nothing to be gained by giving in, when suddenly
anything is possible and the surprising thing is most
possible of all,
Then we remember Him, risen from the dead.

Rise, heart; thy Lord is risen. Sing His praise
Without delays,
Who takes thee by the hand, that thou likewise
With Him mayst rise.

Awake, my lute, and struggle for thy part with all thy art.
The Cross taught all wood to resound His name,
Who love the same,
His stretchèd sinews taught all strings, what key is best
to celebrate this most high day.

MUSIC   Hymn: 'Thine be the glory'

V: Shepherd of the royal flocks
           O Christ our Leader.
2nd V: King of Saints.
V: Word of power, Word of the Father.
2nd V: Father most high.
V: Prince of wisdom, support in all labours,
2nd V: Joy everlasting.

V:	Jesus, the Saviour, Saviour of all.
2nd V:	Shepherd and Husbandman.
V:	Rudder and bridle.
2nd V:	Heavenly wing of the all-holy flock.
V:	Fisher of men.
2nd V:	Haul in Your net.
V:	Gather us safely.
2nd V:	Gather us sweetly.
V:	Out of torrent,
2nd V:	Torrent of danger,
V:	Gather and guard.
2nd V:	Lead us, O Shepherd.
V:	Your flock.
2nd V:	Lead us, O Holy One.
V:	Royal Defender.
2nd V:	Pathway to heaven.
V:	Word everlasting.
2nd V:	World without end.
V:	Light of eternity.
2nd V:	Fountain of mercy.
V:	Jesus, our Christ.

V: Anthony Bloom describes how the Fisher of men gathered him safely – and unexpectedly as the moment when God found him.

I was then a member of a youth organization, a Russian one, and I was invited to come to a talk given by one of our priests. I had no desire to go, but I went and what you expect probably is that I was all of a sudden illumined and convinced. It was not like that at all.

All I heard about Christ, about Christianity, aroused in me a sense of rebellion, or revolt. I found it ugly and disgusting and so, when the talk was over, I went hurriedly home to find out whether what I had heard was true; and I was determined not to waste any more time than needed. I counted the chapters of the Gospels, discovered that the shortest was St Mark's, and set out to read it. I never suspected that the Gospel, St Mark, had been written specially for people of my kind.

What happened next is something which is difficult to describe. I was reading and I suddenly became aware of something which many of you must have felt. The sense that someone is looking at you. The sense that makes you turn in the street to find out what is going on. I felt that there was a presence on the other side of my desk. I looked up and I saw nothing but the sense of this presence was so strong. So overwhelming that I knew it was someone standing on the other side of the desk and further, I became aware that it was the Lord Jesus Christ about whom I was reading. I cannot explain this. The sense of the presence of Christ, real, complete, has remained with me ever since, for more than forty years. I made thus, the basic discovery of Christianity – that Christ was alive. I discovered the mystery of a resurrection of Christ which is at the very root of our faith. As St Paul puts it – 'If Christ is not risen we are the most miserable of all people' because then our faith, our hope, our lives, are founded on a hallucination, on an illusion, on a lie. I discovered then that the resurrection of Christ is the only event of history that belongs both to the past and to the present. It happened in the past and it is real in the present because Christ is in our midst, now as he was and as he shall be.

	Christ is risen!
R:	He is risen indeed!
V:	Christ is raisit!
R:	Atweel He's raisit!
V:	Christ is risen!
R:	He is risen indeed!

For we remember You, O Christ, the Great Reality, the Sun behind all suns: You left Your royal throne, left the realm of light to enter our common paths and grope for us in our darkness. Just for us: common, sly and prickly as we are, to lift us and soothe us and make us clean. We cannot put into words, but we try to say with our lips what we do believe in our hearts, that we really are so grateful that You were born in poverty and not in privilege, that You jostled with evil and with filth and never got contaminated.

Lord Jesus, mystical presence of love, we are so grateful that, when all Your sweetness and forbearance went for nothing, You still climbed onto a cross to make us certain that You really meant it, that for six black hours You danced in agony, with the devil on your back, into black night, and for six black hours all the evil in the world was confronted by You alone and that, after three days, up came the Sun, King Jesus; and You walked and talked again. And the dance went on.

How grateful we are in the perpetual mystery. You are walking and speaking with us now, and what You are Lord of is a dance and not a dirge, so that we too can dance wherever we may be. Therefore, with all the powers that go to make the world, all the forces that keep us alive, we sing to you, with the whole realm of nature, with all the saints, with Columba, with Kentigern, Ninian, who can't really be dead, and with all those who used to worship with us on earth, and with our own friends with whom we used to stand in Church, who now, in the mystery, still stand beside us, they in Your nearer presence, we join with them all singing in our hearts to You: 'Holy, holy, holy ...'

You come to us as we grasp that this bread is vibrant with You, who inhabits all things, and this wine pulsates with You, dark with your continuing sacrifice, and therefore elixir of our spirits and seal of our right to dance ...

Rejoice, heavenly powers! Sing, choirs of angels!
Exult, all Creation round God's throne.
Jesus Christ, our King is risen!
Sound the trumpet of salvation!

Rejoice, O earth, in shining splendour,
Radiant in the brightness of your King!
Christ has conquered! Glory fills you!
Darkness vanishes for ever!

Rejoice, O Mother Church! Exult in glory!
The Risen Saviour shines upon you!
Let this place resound with joy
echoing the mighty song of all God's people!

Father, we praise You.
In the beginning, light came
at Your summoning.
At Your command the green blade
rose from the earth
and became the field.
The bare tree blossomed
into a cascade of leaf.
Men and women were given breath
and speech, room to grow,
freedom to be and to do,
freedom to undo.

Our freedom baffled us.
So: to our bewilderment
You sent the Maker of the great design,
the One in whom, for whom,
by whom, all things hold together – Jesus.

We remember Him.
We commemorate Him.
He is our Light: we summon Him
to shine upon our new perplexities.

He was born for us,
baptized for us,
He taught in our streets,

played with our children,
Argued with the masters
of lore and law, and then left
them speechless. He told stories.
He saw poems everywhere.
He saw possibilities.
He lifted up the fallen,
mended the broken,
pronounced the word of life.

He was captured
and condemned for us.
They nailed Him to the Cross.

But the bare tree blossomed.
Death claimed Him.
But it could not keep Him.
He rose again
and we believe
that he will come again.
Therefore, we sing the ageless hymn,
the song that every citizen of heaven
knows by heart, the song we know
with faith and longing –

MUSIC   *The Sanctus*

V: Glory to You, for Yours
         is the greatness and the power,
         the glory, the splendour, and the majesty.

         There may be someone who says to himself or herself,
         with a sigh: 'Ah, these Christians! They need their
         miracles! Life begins and life ends, that is all. Life is work
         and sleep and shopping; nothing is certain except death
         and taxes. I don't need miracles; I can get by without
         them.'

Walt Whitman says:
'As to me, I know of nothing else but miracles,
Whether I walk the streets of Manhattan
Or dart my sight over the roofs of houses toward the sky,
Or wade with naked feet along the beach just in the edge
of the water,
Or stand under trees in the woods,
Or talk by day with any one I love
Or sleep in the bed at night with any one I love,
Or sit at table at dinner with the rest,
Or look at strangers opposite me riding in the car,
Or watch honey-bees busy round the hive of a summer
forenoon,
Or animals feeding in the fields.
Or birds, or the wonderfulness of insects ...
Or the wonderfulness of sundown ...

These with the rest, one and all, are to me miracles.
To me every hour of the light and dark is a miracle.
Every cubic inch of space is a miracle.
Every square yard of the surface of the earth is spread
with the same,
Every foot of the interior swarms with the same.

To me the sea is a continual miracle,
The fishes that swim – the rocks – the motion of the
waves – the ships with men in them,
What stranger miracles are there?'

Harry Williams says that the secret of life consists not
in our possessing it but in our continually being given it.
The miracle of our being given life beyond the grave is no
greater than the miracle of our continually being given
life here.

MUSIC   'I know that my Redeemer liveth' from *Messiah* by
Handel

156

Love is the Engine of Survival

A prayer

Lord of the powers
present past and to come,
none is beyond you,
none can defeat you,
none can claim they are greater.
Love is the only engine of survival,
and in that knowledge we are secure
for we have never lost you:
Safe in the Father,
safe in the purpose of buying back the world
from the clutches of the king of emptiness
the shackles of the tyrant of terror
the chains of the cheater
who denies God the glory
and tries to take from you
the crown of the king,
the only king we need.

The king of the thorns,
the king of the nails.
And we thought that faith was easy:
We thought that all we had to do
was to be spectators in the drama,
but you ask us to be players
in the gigantic struggle:
Forgive us, we pray, that cowardice
that told us we could hoist the flag

of surrender: that caution that told us
we were off-watch and at ease;
that cosiness of spirit
that said we could let others do the pain
and the protest and the problematical ·
and we could opt out:
'Not possible,
not acceptable'
Lord, have mercy upon us.

We are all meant to be active
from time to time
for God and the kingdom;
and not active only
but anxious for love to survive
the ego-trips and the extremism
of those who think the kingdom
is about them, not the Lord.

Not anxious either but anchored to grace,
founded in grace,
found forever and not ever
to be cast adrift.
not ever (God help us) left
to our own devices, which are often wrong.

Let us be safe in the safety of the king
and when we venture forth
on the enterprises
of our own devising, the low road sometimes
instead of the highway,
Lord bring us home
and tame us into submission to the laws of love
and the high call of that way
where you ask us to be little for you,
big for the path we need to take
as long as it is you who are in front.